D1124216

BATTLE TACTICS
TANK WARFARE

BATTLE TACTICS
TANK WARFARE

Tim Ripley

CASEMATE

Published by
CASEMATE
2114 Darby Road, Havertown, PA 19083

Copyright© Compendium Publishing

ISBN   1-932033-10-6

Cataloging-in-Publication data is available from the Library of Congress.

Printed and bound in Hong Kong
through Printworks Int Ltd.

With Thanks

The author would like to thank the following people for their help providing information, photographs, data and advice, to make this book possible. Joanna Sale and Jonathan Bryne of the DERA Press Office; Stuart Fraser, CDISS; Roddy de Norman, late of the Royal Hussars; Karen Fenwick, of Vickers Defence Systems; Steve Zaloga; Dave Reynolds, DPL; Peter Donnolly, King's Own Regimental Museum; Simon Forty, Compendium Publishing; Teddy Neville, TRH Photographs.

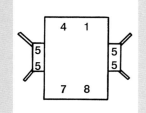

NOTE
The numbers in the crewing diagrams identify:
1. Commander;
2. Gunner; **3.** Loader;
4. Driver; **5.** Hull gunner/ co-driver/radio operator;
6. Hull gunner; **7.** and
8. engine operators.

Page 2: The M4 Sherman may not have been the best tank of World War II, but the sheer number produced made it ubiquitous in the latter stages of the war.

Right: The British Matilda was called the "Queen of the Battlefield" in the early stages of the North African war as no Italian tank or anti-tank guns could penetrate her armor. The arrival of the German 88mm ended this invulnerability and showed up the tactical misconceptions behind production of the "Infantry" tank.

Cover photos: **Background picture, see caption page 133. Inset picture see caption page 13. Back cover picture see caption page 30.**

CONTENTS

INTRODUCTION

"A squadron of our tanks in full cry is enough to strike fear into the hearts of any enemy. Hardly surprising. They're fast, they're flexible, they're survivors. And their firepower is lethal."

That was how a British Army tank commander summed up the battlefield role of the tank in the 21st century. The modern generation of main battle tanks possesses firepower, protection and mobility far in advance of their predecessors that made military history during the combat debut of the tank on the battlefields of the Western Front in 1916. However, the spirit and ethos of those early tank men clearly lives on in the current generation of armored warriors.

This book, the first in a new series on battlefield tactics, looks at the development of tank warfare from the early years of the last century through to the futuristic ideas for the next generation of armored fighting vehicles being proposed today. The emphasis of the book is on how tank crews have fought and survived on the battlefield, relating how technology and tactics have evolved to help tank crews kill their opponents and also to remain alive in supremely hostile environments.

Far left: **Germany's monster Tiger I tank dominated World War II battlefields with its devastating 88mm cannon. Its 100mm thick armor was impervious to most Allied anti-tank guns.**

Left: **Amphibious landings brought thousands of Allied tanks into action during World War II. Here a British Crusader II rehearses for the Dieppe landings in 1942.**

What is a tank?

The word "tank" entered popular usage during World War I after accounts of the first employment of the new armored leviathans were glorified in the newspapers of the era. The name itself originated from the deception campaign organized by the British War Office to hide the true purpose of the vehicles. They were termed "water carriers for Russia" or just "water tanks" as in "tanks, for the storage of water" to try to hide their intended use from the Germans. The first British tracked armored vehicles were in fact initially called "land ships" by the naval officers who designed them, but for reasons lost in the distance of time the name tank stuck and entered common usage.

Tanks are now defined as tracked armored fighting vehicles fitted with 360 degree rotating turrets, which are primarily intended to engage the enemy in direct line of sight combat. They are now but one type of armored vehicle among many, such as armored personnel carriers, self-propelled artillery pieces, armored cars and armored engineer vehicles. In 1916 there was not this plethora of vehicles so any tracked armored vehicle was automatically dubbed a tank, even though they lacked rotating turrets and today would be more likely to be classed as assault guns or self-propelled guns. It was only after World War I that the term tank became associated with this specific type of tracked armored vehicle. Since World War II the term "main battle tank" has come into use to differentiate these machines from reconnaissance vehicles and armored personnel carriers fitted with turrets containing small calibre cannons or heavy machine guns. To the layman these vehicles may appear to be tanks but they are really intended for tasks other than direct combat with the enemy.

Why is it such an important weapon system?

During the last 60 years of the 20th century the tank emerged as a significant weapon in land warfare. It heralded the return of maneuver as the decisive factor in military operations, with Hitler's Panzers spearheading the German *Blitzkrieg* campaigns of 1940 that forever changed the nature of warfare. Almost every country in the world then scrambled to rebuild its army around the tank. Hard hitting offensive tank forces and efficient anti-tank defenses became the main combat components of armies. Land warfare technology revolved around building better tanks or devising new weapons to defeat the enemies' tanks.

Tanks, along with aircraft, missiles and the atom bomb, symbolized a new era of mechanized and industrialized warfare, where a nation's technological

prowess and potential was now decisive. Martial honor and traditions now counted for little in the era of the tank, where a nation's ability to develop heavy armor, high velocity cannons and computerized fire control would sweep all before it.

Why have tanks endured on an ever evolving battlefield?

Ever since the first tanks appeared there have been prophets claiming they would soon be obsolete. First it was the anti-tank gun, followed by the anti-tank mine and then the atomic bomb. In the 1960s and 1970s the

fielding of large numbers of highly accurate anti-tank guided missiles and attack helicopters seemed to herald the death knell of the tank.

The tank has survived all these developments and continued to evolve into an even more powerful weapon system. The concept of a highly mobile armored vehicle, with a powerful armament, has proved to be very enduring. Tanks are just very flexible pieces of military hardware. Their armor means they can risk driving into range of the enemy. Their mobility means they are not dependent on other units or services to maneuver across the battlefield, and can get to the scene of the action under their own power. In war, they

Above: **French Char B1s prepare for battle in 1940 against Hitler's Panzer élite. Although more heavily armored and better armed than their German counterparts, French tanks suffered from poor leadership and logistic support.**

Left: **Italian armor burns in the North African Desert in 1942. The fate of tank crews caught inside destroyed vehicles is far from pleasant.**

countries saw the tank as the answer to the nuclear threat because its armor allowed armies to maneuver across irradiated battlefields with some sort of protection. That at least was the theory. It was never put to the test but the argument was used to justify the continued development and building of tanks during the 1950s and 1960s.

In the modern era, anti-tank guided weapons have not proved to be wonder-weapons and developments in armor and self-defense systems mean the modern tank has a degree of protection unrivalled in its history. This degree of protection is considered essential in the age of "zero-casualty" conflicts. The main threats to the tank are currently proving to be budget cutters in the world's capitals who balk at the huge cost—up to $3.6 million apiece in the case of a U.S. MIAZ Abrams, for example—of modern tanks and their supporting infrastructure. Perhaps the true battlefield worth of tanks will only be recognized when they are gone and the need will arise to reinvent them.

Why are tank crews special?

Ever since the first British tank units were formed in 1916, the men who have fought in tanks have been a unique breed. In World War I tankmen, with their love of mechanical things, were an anathema to many senior officers, particularly those from the cavalry. They were not proper soldiers. How could anyone take pride from tightening a tank track rather than a drill parade, or so

can attack or defend using their own on-board weapon systems. In peacetime, their sheer physical bulk and noise can intimidate opponents without them even having to fire their weapons. Over the past ten years tanks have proved their worth protecting peacekeeping or humanitarian aid missions in hostile environments.

The anti-tank guns of the 1930s and 1940s were just not mobile enough to keep pace with tanks on a fast moving battlefield. Likewise minefields only proved useful in close terrain. In the North African desert or Russian steppe, tanks just drove around them. The atom bomb was supposed to bring an end to the need for large conventional armies. However, many

Above: **On occasions dramatic advances have occurred in tank designs thanks to a few inspired inventors. J. Walter Christie's idea to use large bogie wheels, seen here on a 1930s U.S. Army T4 Combat Car, was one such event.**

Right: **The British Mark IV tank was the first to see combat.**

Far right: **Time and again it has been demonstrated that tanks need the support of specialist vehicles, such as these German SdKfz 250 armored half tracked personnel carriers, to operate effectively on the battlefield.**

thought some of the military dinosaurs who commanded the world's armies in 1916. Tinkering with tanks was a job for the lower orders, not professional army officers, said the aristocratic military men of the era.

Success in battle, however, brought pride and *esprit de corps*. When the newly formed British Tank Corps broke through the German lines at Cambrai in November 1917, a grateful nation ordered church bells to be rung. Technology seemed to offer an answer to the bloody stalemate of the Western Front and the British people took the Tank Corps to their hearts. Likewise, when a young Colonel George Patton of the U.S. Army's Tank Corps returned to New York in March 1919 he was a national celebrity. Try as they might in the years after World War I, the conservative military establishments could not un-invent the new weapon and many ambitious young officers found themselves attracted to the glamor of the tank. In World War II the *Blitzkrieg* victories of Germany's Panzer troops caught the imagination of the world. Other armies sought to turn their armored forces into elite units, as befitting their status at the cutting edge of land power.

The tank crew in itself is a self-contained fighting unit, usually of four or five men. They must work together as a cohesive team for the crew to stand any chance of success and survival in battle. Unlike in the old infantry and artillery of the 19th century, the tank officer is an integral part of the fighting unit. He has to be part of the team. In the cramped interior of a tank turret there is little room for any airs and graces. This closeness brings a unique personal bond that is unknown in other types of unit, except perhaps in a bomber aircraft crew.

Most armies term their tanks as "battle-winning" weapons and employ them at the spearhead of their main combat effort, or *Schwerpunkt* to use German military jargon. This in itself raises the kudos, prestige and morale of tank men. If the fate of their country's military endeavors rests on their shoulders then supreme effort and sacrifice can be expected. In victory, glory goes to those who lead the charge into the enemy's guns.

How tank crews fight their vehicles

In spite of almost a century of development in tank technology the basic roles of a tank crew in the first decade of the 21st century are essentially similar to those in 1916.

The tank commander is obviously in overall command of the vehicle. It is his job to ensure the tank follows the tactical plan laid down by his immediate superior. This essentially involves navigating the tank and passing instructions to the driver. The commander

also has to select targets and give the gunner fire control orders to allow him to move or lay the tank's main armament on target. It may also be necessary to select the type of ammunition to be fired. It is a major part of the commander's job to monitor his tank's technical performance to ensure it is always supplied with ammunition, fuel and other essentials, as well as ensuring the crew carry out any routine maintenance in between operations.

The gunner is responsible for firing the tank's main armament at the targets selected by the commander. He then has to bring his weapon to bear on the target and elevate or drop the gun to ensure it is aimed on the right target. Sighting systems are provided to help him hit the target by correctly judging the range and compensating for wind and other climatic factors. Once a round is fired the gunner has to tell the commander it has hit or fire again, realigning his fall of shot to compensate for any aiming error.

The third member of a tank crew is the driver. His job is largely self explanatory but he is also largely responsible for the close defense of the tank. While the commander and gunner have their eyes set on targets thousands of yards away, it is the driver who is preoccupied with what is happening a few dozen yards

away. Tank driving is not a straightforward skill. The driver must understand intimately how the vehicle's center of gravity affects the way it can drive over hills, to avoid rolling. The weight and width of the tank determine its ability safely to cross bridges or other man-made structures, such as hill or riverside roads. A tank driver must have a sixth sense to spot soft ground, swamps or melting river ice, to ensure he does not get his tank "bogged-in".

Over time tank designs have called for other crew members to fulfil a variety of roles, including hull machine gunners, radio operators and loaders. Their roles are self-evident. Some modern tanks have automatic loaders, eliminating the need for a human loader. Advances in communications technology have also largely negated the need for specialist radio operators. Reduction in crew numbers saves space, reducing the size, shape and weight of the tank, but experienced tank men are always keen not to go below a minimum of four crew members. Human muscle power is needed to change tracks and carry out other essential maintenance. To operate the tank over extended periods in battle also requires the crew to sleep, so a larger crew allows some to rest while the others maintain watch.

Above left: **Tank crews of the 21st century can now learn their trade on virtual reality simulators networked together to recreate virtual battlefields, involving hundreds of players. (STRICOM)**

Above: **Precision guided anti-tank missiles are the tank's most dangerous opponents on the battlefields of the 21st century. (Rafael Armaments Authority)**

Right: **The Leopard 2A5 represents the pinnacle of tank design, combining a powerful 120mm cannon with high levels of protection and excellent mobility. (Krauss-Maffei Wegmann)**

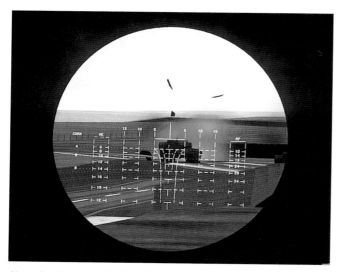

Above: **Another example of a virtual reality simulator.**

Below: **A British Challenger 2 tank. Tanks of the 21st century have powerful powerplants to ensure their massive bulk can maneuver easily across all types of terrain. (Vickers Defence Systems)**

What are the basics of tank tactics?

On the battlefield tanks rarely fight alone. They are combined into groups of three to five tanks known generally as a platoon or troop. Three or four platoons are usually combined into a company or squadron. Several companies or squadrons make up a battalion or regiment, usually the largest size of unit made up solely

of tanks. Larger armored formations generally combine tanks with infantry, anti-tank weapons, engineers or artillery as battlegroups or task forces.

The tactics used by the tank platoon or troop have evolved over time to meet particular battlefield threats or to employ particular weapons. There are a number of core tactical procedures that have remained universal throughout the world's tank crews.

Finding and engaging the enemy in a way that minimizes the chance of the enemy returning fire is still at the heart of tank tactics. Central to tank tactics is use of ground. Young tank commanders are taught from their first days in a turret that their best protection from enemy fire is provided by hills, woods, buildings and bad weather. All these things can be used to hide tanks from the enemy, such as by maneuvering along valley floors rather than driving over or along hill crests. Finding a good firing position is an extension of this skill. Skilful tank commanders will only expose as little of their vehicle as necessary, either to observe or engage the enemy. If necessary, a commander will even dismount and move forward on foot to observe the enemy so as not to expose his tank.

Fire and maneuver is a universal tactic that ensures tank units are never caught unawares by the enemy. Using the principle of "one foot on the ground at all times," pairs or platoons of tanks will take up fire positions to cover their comrades as they move forward. From their "over watch" positions, the reserve tanks will be able pre-emptively to engage any enemy forces that threaten the advancing friendly tanks.

When called upon to close and destroy the enemy, tanks must use their speed and mass to full advantage. Tanks are large, noisy and threatening. By presenting their heavy frontal armor to the enemy, tanks minimize their vulnerability during the final phase of an assault. There is nothing more terrifying to an enemy infantryman or anti-tank gunner than a seemingly impregnable armored monster advancing at full speed towards him, firing on the move. Once tanks close with the enemy, their rotating turrets come into their own allowing targets to be engaged on either side of the vehicles as they move through the enemy's defense lines. In close-quarter battles, the tank's tracks become weapons, crushing enemy bunkers or trenches.

It is in this phase of battle that the tank's unique characteristics come into their own. No other weapon system combines the mobility, firepower and armored protection necessary to advance into the heart of the enemy's defenses, spreading terror and chaos in its wake. For this reason a replacement for the tank is difficult to imagine.

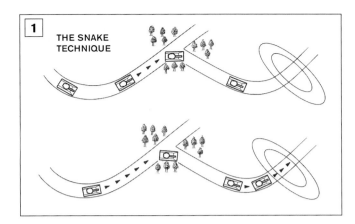

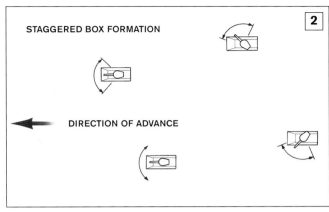

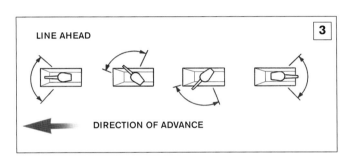

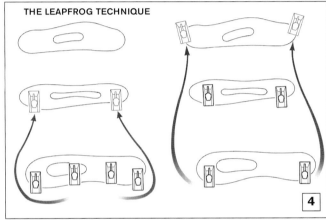

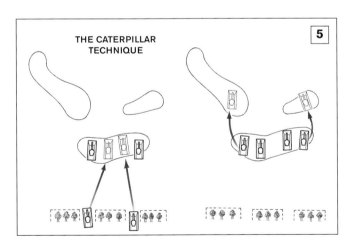

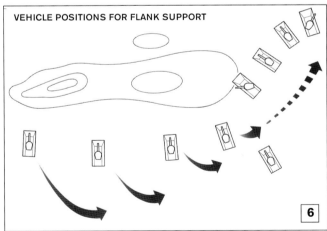

TECHNIQUES FOR ADVANCING TO CONTACT

1. The snake technique sees vehicles shuffle forward, each vehicle moving under the protection of the next.

2. Staggered box formation shows a direct advance with arcs of fire.

3. Line ahead advance showing arcs of fire.

4. The leapfrog technique, two vehicles cover while the next two advance.

5. In the caterpillar technique, the advance is less ambitious and more careful.

6. Vehicle positions for flank support.

The Battlefield

For the soldiers manning the opposing trench lines of the Western Front in late 1914 and into 1915, the idea that World War I would be brought to a swift conclusion was a fantasy. Their daily fight for survival against artillery, machine guns, barbed-wire entanglements, poison gas, rain and mud seemed never ending. They would count an advance of a few yards as a major success and then it would be paid for in blood. The loss of thousands of casualties during seemly pointless offensives had become almost routine. In one phase of the Battle of Loos, in September 1915, some 10,000 British Tommies went over the top. A few hours later, less than 2,000 returned safely to the British trenches. The remainder of the attacking troops were slaughtered by German machine guns and artillery fire. German commanders reported no casualties in that sector of the front that day.

This lamentable state of affairs was not supposed to happen. When the war broke out in August 1914 the high commands of all the major armies envisaged a high-tempo war of maneuver and encirclement. Cavalry corps and divisions would surge around the flanks of the enemy in almost Napoleonic-style sweeps. In the early weeks of the war the promises of maneuver seemed likely to be fulfilled. The German offensive into France, via Belgium, swept all before it just as the great General von Schlieffen had predicted. Barely a month later the Germans were in retreat, their attempt to capture Paris being thwarted on the River Marne. When the opposing armies did meet in battle, the casualties to machine guns and artillery were horrendous. Whole battalions of infantry were cut down as they tried to advance across country to bayonet charge the enemy. Cavalry shared a similar fate when it attempted to close to sabre slashing distance.

By the end of the year the Western Front had stabilized. It would remain largely static for more than three years. To escape the torrent of shells and bullets that engulfed the battlefield, the British, French and German armies started digging. The frontline positions of the opposing armies disappeared underground into bunkers and trench lines, that stretched all the way from the English Channel coast to the Swiss border. Huge barbed-wire entanglements and obstacles were created to delay the enemy's advance and trap them in the open in no-man's-land to be slaughtered by machine-gun and artillery fire. Initial attempts to break through these lines were repulsed with great losses, as at Loos. It was decided that new tactics and weapons would be needed to break the stalemate. The Germans turned to their scientists, who fielded the first poison gas in 1915. They then sought to develop new tactics to break open the enemy frontline by guile. This was the origin of the famous stormtrooper or infiltration tactics that brought the Germans success on battlefields in the east in 1917 and in the west in spring 1918. For most of the war the Germans were happy to remain on the defensive in the west, allowing the Allies to suffer horrendous losses trying to breach their defenses. During 1915 and 1916 the Germans started to create concrete bunkers and firing positions to increase further the strength of their defenses.

The British and French turned to artillery to open the way forward for their infantry. Huge barrages of artillery fire were to saturate the enemy defenses, destroying enemy machine-gun posts and opening routes through the barbed-wire entanglements. The infantry would then advance under the cover of a so-called rolling barrage of shells that was intended to protect them until they could surge into the enemy's trenches and put them to flight at bayonet point. Once the infantry had taken control of the enemy's trenches, divisions of cavalry were to move forward to exploit the breach in the enemy line, fanning out to attack supply dumps, artillery positions and headquarters.

Theory, however, bore little resemblance to reality. Allied artillery fire could never account for 100% of the German defenders. There were always just enough German machine gunners alive after a bombardment to wreak havoc among the advancing Allied infantry. The rolling barrage was a fundamentally flawed concept. It relied on a strict timetable to schedule its move forward. The technology just did not exist to allow Allied gunners to zero in their artillery fire on a particular point on the battlefield during a fast moving battle, such as a German machine-gun nest that was holding up the advance.

The July 1916 Somme offensive highlighted these weaknesses and the British attack was repulsed with heavy losses. Reliance on heavy artillery barrages proved to be counter-productive. It churned up the ground and created a muddy moonscape that was almost impassable by infantry once the fall rains began. The prospect of a decisive breakthrough looked very remote. Allied cavalry divisions were gradually disbanded and their manpower drafted into the trenches to bolster the hard pressed infantry.

Events on the Eastern Front, in the Balkans and in the Mid-East were far from rosy for the Allies. Russia was on the verge of revolution. German, Austrian and Turkish troops were in the ascendant, defeating attempts to defeat the Central Powers decisively away from the Western Front, such as the British landing at Gallipoli. The outcome of the war would be decided on the Western Front.

Tank Technology

As the dismal state of affairs on the Western Front became known to British political and military leaders, there was a demand for a solution to break the stalemate. Imaginative thought was not a strong point of the British Army's senior leadership, which had learned its trade in colonial conflicts against native troops and was largely out of its depth fighting a major European war.

Civilian politicians, industrialists and naval officers by different routes all came to the conclusion that armored vehicles could be used as weapons of war. The Royal Navy had formed its first armored car units in the

Below: **Rolls-Royce armored cars were the first armored vehicles to see service with the British in World War I but the Royal Naval Air Service soon found they had limited cross country mobility.**

first months of the war to fight alongside its aircraft squadrons in Belgium. However, wheeled armored cars were just not able to maneuver off-road in the dreadful conditions of the Western Front, so a new solution was required.

British and French artillery units were already using a vehicle called the Holt tractor to move guns into firing positions. They used a track laying device to travel across country. By driving a continuous loop of linked metal track, rather than wheels, tracked vehicles were able to cross types of terrain that was impassable to other types of vehicle.

Naval influence remained strong and the War Office formed a committee to develop what were then called "Land Ships." The British Army's high command in France displayed no enthusiasm for the new weapon.

Experiments in track, transmission and armor took place during the second half of 1915 and the first British tank, nicknamed *Little Willie*, demonstrated that it was possible to build a viable armored vehicle. This was little more than a metal box, with poor trench crossing capabilities and no armament. The next progression was the famous rhomboid-shaped design that was first known as *Centipede*, then *Big Willie* and *Mother*. It became the benchmark design for British tanks in World War I, thanks to its gun turrets or sponsons on either side of its hull containing 6-pounder (57mm) guns or machine guns. *Mother* ran on its tracks during trials on 16th January 1916 and within weeks the War Office ordered 100 under the designation Mark I.

It was a very rudimentary design to say the least. The 31 U.S. tons Mark I's transmission was primitive, and it relied on a pair of tail wheels for steering. The seven man crew had to work in such a noisy and cramped compartment, that the only way for them to communicate with each other was by a system of hand signals. When the armament was fired the inside of the vehicle filled with noxious fumes. The commander sat in the front of the vehicle in a small raised armored box between the front of the tracks and could only see forward out of narrow slits, protected by fold-up armored hatches. To direct the fire of his gunners, the commander had to leave his position and physically move to shout in their ears.

Over the next two years the design went through considerable evolution until the final wartime rendition, the Mark VII, which featured hydraulic transmission, electric starters and cooling systems. The most famous and most numerous version was the Mark IV which led the 1917 Cambrai offensive. Specialist versions of the Mark IV included supply carriers, radio equipped vehicles, telephone cable layers, searchlight carriers, infantry transports, mine "exploders" or clearers and

Above: **The mud of the Western Front hindered mobility until tracked designs were available in large numbers in 1917–18.**

Above right: **The Mark IV with its distinctive track lay-out and side sponsons was the British Army's main tank during World War I.**

engineering tanks. In total more than 2,000 versions of the basic British tank were built during the war. Trench crossing was a major part of the tanks' work and the British soon equipped many of theirs with fascines, or bundles of logs, to be dropped into wide or deep trenches to provide an improvised crossing.

The British worked on a variety of designs during the war, the majority of which never saw action. A 100-ton heavy tank was just beyond the technical capability of British industry, not to mention impossibly large and un-maneuverable. Effort was concentrated on building a fleet of some 200 125.7 U.S. ton medium tanks, called the Medium A or Whippet. This was a "cheap and cheerful" design armed only with machine guns, but its 8mph was twice that of the Mark I. This mobility allowed British tank commanders to think of their machines as more than just close assault weapons to support infantry attacks.

Name: Mark IV "Male"

Designer/Manufacturer: Foster & Company

Weight: 28/31.3 tons (28.5 tonnes)

Main armament: 2 x 6-pdr (57mm)

Secondary armament: 4 x machine guns

Powerplant: 105hp Daimler gasoline

Frontal armor: 12mm

Hull length: 32ft 6in (9.9m)

Width: 13ft 9in (4.19m)

Height: 8ft 0in (2.43m)

Speed: 4mph (9km/hr)

Crew: 8

Date entered service: 1916

Claim to fame: First tank to see combat

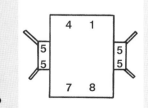

Working independently from the British, the French also turned to the Holt tractor as the basis for their first tank designs. The first French vehicles, the 13.5-ton Schneider M16 and 23-ton St Chamond M16, had very poor trench-crossing capabilities because their hulls overhung in front of and behind their tracks. They easily became stuck crossing trenches and ended up as sitting ducks for German artillery. Although the St Chamond had a powerful 75mm gun mounted in its front compartments, it had a very limited angle of traverse. Some 400 of each design were built during the war.

The next French design, the 7-ton Renault FT 17, was far more successful and more than 3,000 were built. It had a rotating turret, which meant it could bring its 37mm gun or machine gun to bear against targets off to its side. This useful little tank was adopted by the American Expeditionary Force in 1917, along with British tanks, until the production of tanks in the United States could get underway. Joint development of new U.S.-British heavy tanks was slow in starting and the U.S. Army had to rely on foreign-made tanks until the end of the war.

Name: FT 17
Designer/Manufacturer:
Renault
Weight: 6.9/7.7 tons
(7 tonnes)
Main armament:
1 x 37mm
Secondary armament: 1 x machine gun
Powerplant: 35hp Renault gasoline
Frontal armor: 22mm
Hull length: 16ft 5in (5m)
Width: 5ft 9in (1.74m)
Height: 6ft 7in (2.14m)
Speed: 5mph (8km/hr)
Crew: 2
Date entered service: 1917
Claim to fame: First tank
with rotating turret

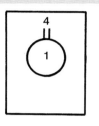

German interest in tanks was late in developing and by the end of World War I only 20 tanks had been produced for the Kaiser's army. However, scores of captured British Mark IVs were eventually pressed into German service. The only home-designed and produced German tank was designated the A7V. It drew on both British and French designs, with a frontally mounted 57mm main gun and six side- and rear-mounted heavy machine guns. It had a staggering 20-man crew to operate its complicated machinery and numerous weapons.

As the nation on the receiving end of the first ever tank attacks, the Germans were in the forefront of the development of anti-tank weapons. Their most effective defense against the tank was the armor-piercing bullet for machine guns. These bullets, which could be fired by standard machine guns, were originally developed to punch through the metal plates used to protect allied machine-gun firing positions in trench lines. They were simply made by using hardened metal rather than the traditional soft alloys previously used in small arms ammunition. When these bullets were used to rake Allied tanks they rarely caused serious damage, usually passing straight in and out of the vehicles, but did cause heavy casualties among the crews. One surprise discovery was the effectiveness of high velocity German anti-aircraft guns against tanks. Trucks mounting 77mm anti-aircraft guns were drafted in as an emergency

measure to counter British tanks during the Battle of Cambrai and were such a success that the Germans retained the idea, leading eventually to the employment of the famous 88mm Flak guns in the anti-tank role in World War II.

Tactical and Doctrinal Development

The tactics of armored warfare went through a very rapid evolution after the new British tanks went into action for the first time on September 15, 1916. Early tank pioneers, such as Ernest Swinton of the British Army's newly formed Tank Corps and the then unknown Lieutenant Colonel George Patton of the U.S. Army, had little idea what would happen when their machines faced enemy fire. They developed complicated concepts for crossing trenches and other maneuvers. These envisaged trios of tanks working together, with two tanks parked side-on providing covering fire from their sponson guns while the third tank placed its fascine in the enemy trench and moved across. It would then cover its two colleagues as they crossed over the fascine.

Right: **The British developed a number of specialist tanks to support their combat vehicles in World War I, including supply tanks to replenish fuel and ammunition so the momentum of an advance could be maintained. Note absence of armamant in sponsons.**

Below left: **The Renault FT 17 was the first tank to be fitted with a 360-degree rotating turret. It was the most successful French tank of the war, with more than 4,000 being built.**

At this stage in the development of the tank, the idea that tanks would fight independently of infantry was not considered. They were just not technologically mature enough to move at anything faster than a walking pace across the battlefields of France. British tanks were considered primarily as infantry support weapons, advancing with the infantry to clear the way forward for them by breaching enemy barbed-wire entanglements and engaging any enemy machine guns. During the brief spells of tank action during the later days of the Battle of the Somme in 1916, infantry tank co-operation developed considerably. Infantry learned to hang back, just behind the tanks, allowing their armored escorts to engage in duels with pockets of enemy resistance. Once the tanks had crossed the enemy trench lines, the infantry would drop down into the trenches and clear out the defenders at bayonet point.

Tank crews had an almost non-existent view of the battlefield, so close infantry co-operation was essential to pinpoint targets for the tank's guns. Early tank commanders rarely rode into battle inside their tanks. They preferred to ride on the back or walk alongside the infantry to allow them to get a good view of the battlefield. Once a target was identified the commander would run to the nearest tank to give its crew their orders. All engagements were at very short range, well under 400 yards, because of the primitive nature of the tank's weapon sights. Any thought of accurately engaging any type of target while on the move was out of the question for the same reason. The lack of effective communications between tanks meant that early ideas for co-ordinated action proved unworkable on the battlefield. Those pioneering tank commanders learned the hard way that they had to lead from the front.

Early tanks of all nationalities proved terribly mechanically temperamental and, on average, crews could expect them to remain operational for little more than a day, before they had to pull back for repairs and maintenance. This, more than anything, limited the ambitions of early tank warfare theorists. The long range mobility of armored forces was also limited because of the small size of their fuel tanks and heavy fuel consumption. The British used rail transports to give their tanks strategic mobility but the French tried to extend the range of their tanks by loading extra fuel tanks on their cabin roofs. These turned the tanks into death traps when German artillery zeroed in on them during the battle along the Aisne in April 1917, destroying 32 out of 48 St Chamonds committed and incinerating their crews inside them.

During their first engagements, the British tanks spread panic and confusion among the German troops. Once their machine guns failed to stop the armored monsters, the German infantry were soon overtaken with "tank terror" and they fled in large numbers. However, experience soon taught the Germans that the

British tanks had major limitations in terms of their ability to find targets and co-operate with infantry.

The Germans learned to hold their fire until the British tanks were moving past or across their trench lines. They would then emerge and start taking on the British infantry. More often than not, the tanks had little idea what was going on behind them and would continue driving forward. Unaccompanied by infantry the tanks were soon "blind." This was the point at which the German field guns or anti-aircraft guns would be brought into the action. The German gunners had better visibility than their opponents and could easily mass fire against individual tanks. The slow speed of the Allied tanks meant that German gunners were often able to engage them leisurely with little risk of retaliation. On one occasion it took a German gun crew 25 shots to put a British Mark IV out of action but during this time the tank crew were largely oblivious to the fact they were under fire and did not manage to fire off a single round at the German guns. Once they were isolated inside the enemy defensive position without infantry support it was only a matter of time before the Germans picked off the Allied tanks one by one. British tanks crews became expert at dismounting and fighting as infantry in such circumstances. In these cases, the large crews of World War I era tanks came into their own.

The British tank pioneers were convinced that the way to compensate for the deficiencies of their primitive vehicles was to employ tanks *en masse*. This way the German defenses would be overwhelmed and the enemy gunners would not be able to concentrate against small groups of tanks. Field Marshal Sir Douglas Haig, the British commander-in-chief in France, decided to give the Tank Corps its wish on November 20, 1917, at Cambrai. More than 378 tanks, mostly Mark IVs, were massed for the action, which was to be preceded by a surprise artillery barrage and extensive air support. The presence of the tanks allowed a strong force of British infantry to make a massive break-in into the German Hindenburg Line fortifications for what, at the time, were minimal

Far Left: **Good cooperation with infantry was the key to the successful employment of tanks during World War I.**

Left and Below: **Two more views of the FT 17.**

casualties. By massing their tanks, the British armor was able swiftly to overcome the German defenses and push on. Where tank-infantry co-operation was good the Germans were unable to stop the advance or more importantly inflict casualties on the British. The tanks quickly destroyed any targets pin-pointed by the infantry. In other parts of the battlefield the tanks and infantry became separated and the advance stalled. By the end of November 20 a four-mile deep penetration of the German line was made and 5,000 prisoners taken for the loss of only a few hundred British dead. The tanks were just not up to the job of exploiting the breach in the Hindenburg Line, however, and the Germans were soon able to counterattack. By the end of the first day of the battle, 179 tanks were out of action and three days later only 92 tanks were fit for action. The remainder had either been knocked out or broken down on the battlefield. The Tank Corps was withdrawn from action after a week of fighting.

Below and Right and Over page: **The first French Schneider tanks went into action in April 1917. They proved to have very limited trench crossing capabilities.**

Cambrai ended in a strategic stalemate, but it showed the potential of the tank decisively to alter the tactical balance on the Western Front. Immediately the British reinvigorated their efforts to build more and better tanks, with improved mobility, armor, armament and communications. Tanks were increasingly integrated into Allied battle plans during the final year of the war, but tank technology and tactics did not significantly advance by the time the Armistice was called in November 1918.

Experience of Battle

For the tank pioneers of the British Tank Corps, such as the then Colonel Percy Hobart, developing effective tactics was no easy matter. By the time of Cambrai, they were convinced that the massing of hundreds of tanks was the way to compensate for the mechanical weaknesses of the early machines. Hobart wrote:

"*As the tanks could not maneuver to take advantage of the situations as they arose, each machine had to be given a definite and limited objective and definite job to*

carry out. To make sure no ground which held a machine gun was left uncovered, the whole front to be attacked had to be covered by the tanks. Each tank fought an individual and isolated combat without much hope of assistance from its brothers except by chance, and numbers had to make up for lack of control and power of maneuver." [1]

The sole purpose of tanks was to help the infantry get through the enemy without suffering heavy casualties. One Tank Corps' officer explained the effect of barbed wire on British tanks in the opening hours of the Battle of Cambrai:

"It [the wire] *neither stopped the tank nor broke up and wound round and round the tracks as we first feared, but squashed flat and remained flat, leaving a broad carpet of wire as wide as the tank over which the following infantry were able to pick their way without great difficulty."*

The officers and men of the Tank Corps were highly motivated to succeed during Cambrai. They saw the battle as the chance to prove the worth of their machines to a still sceptical British Army. Their commander, Brigadier Hugh Elles, issued his famous Special Order No 6 to his crews on the eve of the battle, declaring:

"Tomorrow the Tank Corps will have the chance for which it has been waiting for many months to operate on good going in the van of the battle. All that hard work and ingenuity can achieve has been done in the way of preparation. It remains for unit commanders and tank crews to complete the work by judgement and pluck in the battle itself. In the light of the past experience I leave the good name of the Corps with great confidence in your hands. I propose leading the attack of the Centre Division." [2]

The brigadier was true to his word and mounted his battle standard on a Mark IV which rolled forward with the first assault wave. The young Tank Corps' officers, in particular, were inspired by the commander's example and led the attack with great determination and panache. Second Lieutenant W.P. Whyte left a good account of the action during the first hours of the battle:

"Tank 2882 being hopelessly ditched I at once took over Tank 2877 with the crew of C34 as 2nd Lieutenant Row had just been wounded. Went to the right of Bleak House into the hollow south west of Pam Pam Farm. Silenced two machine guns then turned north to Pam Pam Farm. Just as we swung north two vision plates got blown in with machine-gun fire and two of the crew badly wounded, also two machine guns knocked out leaving us with only one gun. As no infantry could be seen I returned and got in touch with them ... I dumped the wounded and again proceeded to the right of the Pam Pam Farm where machine guns holding up infantry. I cleared that lot out and got on to the Brown line (the secondary objective) by 11am. Here our last gun got over heated and seized leaving us helpless ... An enemy battery got on us and blew in the door and a hole in the tracks and bullets came in where the vision plates should have been and punctured the return water pipes. This we patched and as all our guns were useless I thought it best to rally. This we did and on our way back pulled 2nd Lieutenant Morris's tank which had got badly ditched. We got to R 17 Central about 2pm. The ground was excellent and also trenches." [3]

Early success of the attack boosted morale according to Lieutenant T.A. Crouch:

"I was in one of those [tanks during Cambrai] and the whole thing was the most extra-ordinary operation I have seen or heard of. The Bosche simply ran for his life." [4]

This young officer was soon awarded the Distinguished Service Order for his actions on November 20, leading his section of three tanks. His D.S.O. citation read:

"On arrival of the [Crouch's] *tanks in Marcoing without infantry support this officer's conduct was most gallant. He moved across the open space on foot, all alone under heavy machine-gun fire and succeeded in getting his tanks through the village."*

The Tank Corps' C Battalion, however, met serious opposition from German gun batteries, positioned to cover the village of Flesquières, which began to pick off the slow moving British tanks. A tank crewman, Corporal W.T. Dawson, recalled:

"On the right of Flesquières on top of a ridge were about a dozen or so of E Battalion tanks knocked out. They extended on a line which would be about 150 yards and presented a ghastly sight not only knocked out but some hit by four or five shells, being complete smashed—tracks standing up in the air and burnt out… " [5]

In other parts of the battlefield, the British tanks out-ran their infantry support with potentially disastrous results. One survivor of the battle recounted that:

"On the edge of Fontaine village 2nd Lieutenant A. Mustard's tank was attacking with No 9 Section. On reaching the outskirts of the village, his tank experienced engine trouble and stopped. The tank was surrounded by enemy who bombed it and fired at point blank range through the gun mountings and loopholes, three of his gunners being wounded. He was called upon by the enemy to surrender, but ordering his gunners to keep up Lewis gun fire, he himself worked at the engine and after three quarters of an hour succeeded in starting it and finally brought his tank out of action."

On April 24, 1918, the first recorded tank versus tank engagement occurred when three German A7Vs led a regiment of infantry to attack the British held village of Villers-Bretonneux. Three British tanks, one a gun-armed Mark IV "Male" and two machine-gun-armed Mark IV "Females," happened to be operating near the village. [6]

Lieutenant F. Mitchell commander of the Mark IV "Male" recalled that he was not expecting an enemy tank attack:

"We zigzagged undamaged through a very heavy barrage, reaching the switch line at about 9.30am. An infantryman jumped out of a trench in front of my tank and waved a rifle agitatedly. I slowed down and opened the flap. 'Look out, there are Jerry tanks about,' he shouted. This was my first intimation the Germans were using tanks. I gazed ahead and saw three weirdly shaped objects moving towards the eastern edge of Cachy, one about 400 yards away and the other two being much further away to the south. Behind the tanks I could see lines of advancing infantry.

Right: **The Germans only produced one tank which saw action during World War I. The A7V was slow, overweight and was not a success. This example fell into British hands in 1918.**

Far right: **The open and exposed nature of Western Front battlefields resulted in millions of infantrymen dying during hopeless offensives. Tanks offered a way to transverse this moonscape under armored protection.**

"I was travelling more or less parallel to the nearest German tank and my left hand gunner began to range on it. The first shots went beyond but he soon ranged nearer. I noticed no reply from the German tank. My attention was now fully fixed on the German tank nearest to me, which was moving slowly. The right hand gunner was firing steadily but as I kept continuously zigzagging and there were many shell holes, accurate shooting was not possible. Suddenly there was a noise like a storm of hail beating against our right wall and the tank became alive with splinters. It was a broadside of armor-piercing bullets from the German tank. The crew lay flat on the floor. I ordered the driver to go straight ahead and we gradually drew clear but our faces were splintered. Steel helmets protected our heads."

The out-gunned "Female" tanks were both holed and pulled back to safety, leaving Mitchell to re-engage the German tanks:

"I continued carefully on my route in front of the switch line. The left hand gunner was now shooting well. His shells were bursting very near to the German tank. I opened the loophole at the top side of the cab for better observation and when opposite our opponent, we stopped. The gunner ranged steadily nearer and then I saw a shell burst high up on the forward part of the German tank. It was a direct hit. He obtained a second hit almost immediately lower down the side facing us and then a third in the same region. It was splendid shooting for a man whose eyes were swollen with gas and who was working his gun single handed, owing to shortage of crew.

"The German tank stopped abruptly and tilted slightly. Men ran out of the door at the side and I fired at them with my Lewis gun. The German infantry following behind stopped also. The other two German tanks now gradually drew nearer and seemed to make in my direction. We kept shooting at the nearer

*one, our shells bursting all round it, when suddenly both
tanks slowly withdrew and disappeared."* [6]

The Germans, however, had no idea they had come
under attack by British tanks and returned to base
unaware of the second engagement with Mitchell's
tank, believing their loss to be due to British artillery
fire.

American tank commanders and crews were just as
determined to succeed as their British counterparts.
Lieutenant Colonel George Patton was in command of
the 1st Tank Brigade and, prior to the first engagement
of his unit of Renault FT 17s in the September 1918
Saint Mihiel offensive, he issued a rousing order to his
troops:

*"If you are left alone in the midst of the enemy keep
shooting. If your gun is disabled use your pistols and
squash the enemy with your tracks… remember that you
are the first American tanks. You must establish the fact
that AMERICAN TANKS DO NOT SURRENDER
… as long as one tank is able to move it must go
forward. Its presence will save the lives of hundreds of
infantry and kill many Germans … This is our BIG
CHANCE; WHAT WE HAVE WORKED FOR …
MAKE IT WORTHWHILE.'* [7]

Like his British counterparts, Patton led his tanks
into action sitting on top of the lead tank. In his after-
action report he recounted the experience when they
came under enemy fire for the first time:

*"We continually expected to be shot off our precarious
perch. At the north end of the town we saw one
German. Lieutenant Knowles and Sergeant Graham,
the runner, got off the tank to affect capture. To their
great surprise they found thirty instead of one but using
their pistols they captured the entire crew. The tank
continued to the north end of the town… Colonel
Patton, who was still standing on top of the tank, here,
had the most horrible experience: he could hear machine
gun fire but could not locate them until glancing down
the left side of the tank about six inches below his hand
he saw paint flying from the side of the tank as the
result of numerous bullets striking against the tank.
Owing to his heroic desire to make the tank a less
enticing target he leaped from the tank and landed in a
shell hole a great distance away. This hole, however, was*

Right and Over page: **The American Expeditionary Force used the Renault
FT 17 in large numbers during its offensives in France during 1918.**

exceedingly small and the Germans took an unpleasant delight in shooting at its upper rim."

Patton's tanks met limited resistance during the Saint Mihiel battle but during the Meuse-Argonne offensive from 26th September the Germans fought hard to stop the American tanks breaking through their thick defense lines. As in the previous battle Patton led from the front. This time heavy fire stalled Patton's

attack and he found himself pinned down under heavy enemy fire with his tanks. He recalled that the tanks were:

"A dangerously large target to the enemy. However, before they registered on the spot, the tanks scattered behind cover. Two French Schneider tanks persisted in pushing forwards and were stalled in the only other crossing over the trench systems." [8]

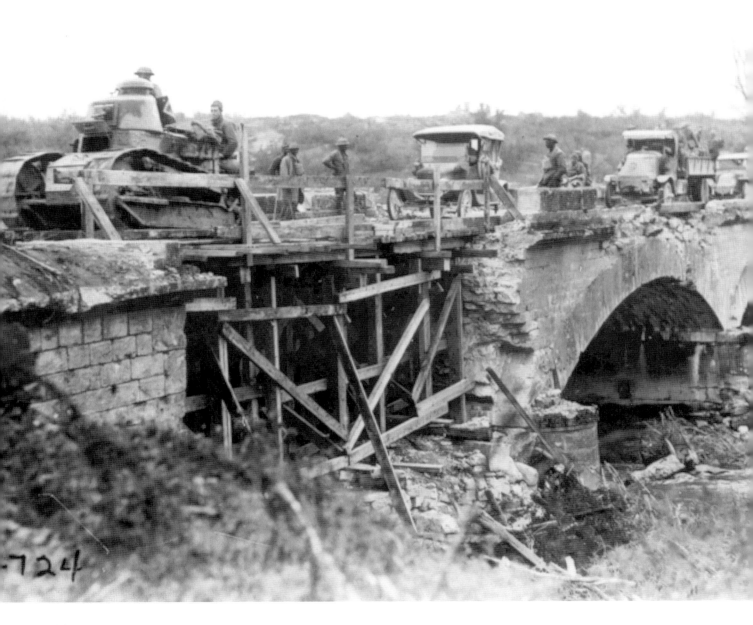

Lieutenant Paul Edwards, Patton's signals officer, described how the Colonel organized getting the tanks across the German trenches:

"[Patton] *went over to the tanks which were being splattered with machine gun fire and removed the shovels and picks and put the men to work. In spite of the repeated requests that he step down in the trench from his exposed position the Colonel steadfastly refused to do so saying, 'To Hell, with them—they can't hit me.' There were a number of casualties among those who were tearing down the sides of the trenches for the passage of the tanks but the Colonel refused to budge.*"

Patton's batman, Private Joseph Angelo, continues the story:

"*In a few minutes the tanks began to move forward over the hill where small groups of infantry had taken cover in shell craters. The Colonel asked an infantry sergeant if there were any of his officers present, to which he answered no. The Sergeant then asked Colonel Patton what he should do and he replied 'follow me.'*"

A few minutes later Patton's luck ran out and he was hit by a stray machine-gun bullet in the upper thigh. The future World War II general had to be evacuated from the battlefield but the American attack could now progress.

Few could claim that tanks had won World War I for the Allies. Nevertheless, the Battle of Cambrai and subsequent tank engagements in 1918 had demonstrated clearly the potential of the tank to return maneuver to the battlefield.

The Battlefield

The horrendous losses incurred by all sides in World War I shaped the world for the next twenty years. The war was described in the popular press of the time as the "war to end all wars." All the major European countries were exhausted, both physically and psychologically, by the four-year-long conflict. The huge armies that had fought the war were rapidly demobilized and the armaments industries built up to fuel the conflict were also switched to civilian production. The prospect of another European conflict seemed so remote that the British, pioneers of the tank in World War I, based their foreign and defense policy on the basis that there would not be another war for at least 10 years. This was the infamous "10 Year Rule." The United States also cut defense spending to the bone and followed a strictly isolationist foreign policy.

The British and the French became preoccupied with minor colonial conflicts during the 1920s, while the Germans were prohibited by the terms of the Treaty of Versailles from having an army greater than 100,000 men. This treaty also prohibited the Germans from possessing tanks, a general staff and an air force in a bid to prevent future "aggression" by Berlin. For most of the 1920s, this state of affairs prevailed with little to disturb the peace. The western world was not interested in wars and more concerned about the state of its stock markets.

In Russia, the new Soviet regime was struggling to rebuild the shattered country in the aftermath of World War I and the country's own bloody Civil War. The Soviet leaders were steeped in revolutionary Communist ideology and remained convinced that they would soon have to fight a war of survival against the capitalist West. They began a crash program of industrialization to ensure their country could build the weapons needed in this conflict.

Germany's much reduced army and right wing nationalist politicians continued to harbor resentment against the terms of the Versailles Treaty that had reduced their military potential, and stripped the country of territory in the east and along its western border, as well as forcing the demilitarization of the Rhineland. The foundations of a covert rearmament plan were laid in the 1920s, including a secret treaty between the Germany military, the *Reichswehr*, and the Soviet Union to co-operate to develop tanks, aircraft and poison gas. The accession to power of Adolf Hitler and his Nazi Party, in 1933, led Germany to repudiate the Versailles restrictions in 1935. Germany soon stepped up its program of rearmament to support Hitler's aggressive foreign policy.

In response Britain, France and the United States all set in train military expansion programs later in the 1930s, but they were nowhere near the scale of those being pursued by Germany, Italy, Japan and Russia. When the world was engulfed by war again in 1939 the western powers would be at a serious disadvantage.

Tactical and Doctrinal Development

The British, as the pioneers of tank warfare, retained a strong interest in developing the tank's potential, even

Bottom left: **The heavily armored French Char B1 was considered the best tank to emerge during the 1930s but proved poorly matched against more mobile German tanks during the 1940 invasion of France.**

Left: **A Vickers Medium of the Royal Tank Corps during the famous Mechanized Force experimental maneuvers in the late 1920s.**

if there was little money available to mass produce new tanks themselves. The Tank Corps remained in existence and was granted the Royal title in 1923. World War I veterans such as Ernest Swinton, J.F.C. Fuller, Giffard le Q. Martel and Hugh Elles remained enthusiastic tank exponents during the lean years of the 1920s and early 1930s. They expounded visions of tank armies making the decisive breakthrough of the enemy's front and then penetrating deep into his rear area. Their "model" tank armies would contain not just tanks but whole families of armored and motorized vehicles to carry infantry, artillery, supplies and engineering equipment and to conduct reconnaissance.

In 1927 the Royal Tank Corps assembled an experimental Mechanised Force on Salisbury Plain for the first ever large-scale armored exercise. The experience became almost an annual event, with new vehicles and equipment being debuted every year. British tank commanders were particularly keen to test the use of their armored force with radios and the exercises of 1931 saw the first ever attempt to

command a brigade-sized force entirely by radio. The Mechanised Force ran rings round its conventionally controlled enemy, heralding a major advance in military science.

During the 1930s the British Army senior leadership, however, drew some unfortunate lessons from the mechanized experiments. It concluded that a special force of fast so-called "cruiser" tanks was needed to engage enemy tanks, while less mobile and more heavily armored "infantry" tanks took on support for the rest of the army. These "I" tanks were not required to have the capability to engage the enemy's armor only his infantry defenses with machine guns. This led to British tank designs being out-classed when they had to meet German designs capable of multi-role work. In the late 1930s the British grouped all their cruiser tanks into an armored division. It was envisaged that this division would operate ahead of the main British force, engaging enemy tanks.

French tank doctrine did not progress much beyond its World War I state during the 1930s, as the nation became preoccupied with building the massive Maginot Line fortifications along the border with Germany. Infantry support work remained the only battlefield mission of French tanks. The French eventually formed light mechanized divisions but they had a cavalry-scouting role.

In the United States tank enthusiasts were cast aside in 1920 when the Tank Corps was abolished and all tanks transferred to the Infantry. Many of the early tank pioneers, such as Colonel George Patton, transferred to the Cavalry, where some experiments in mechanization were allowed to continue, with the 7th Cavalry Brigade (Mechanized) being formed in 1931. The Cavalry was forbidden by law from owning or operating tanks, however, so the vehicles used had to be given the title Combat Cars. It would not be until 1940 that the Armored Force would re-emerge as an independent branch of the U.S. Army.

Japan also had a strong interest in tanks. It bought several foreign tanks to copy and then build in its own factories. By the late 1930s the Japanese had formed three tank divisions and several independent tank brigades. The country's island geography and the jungle terrain of much of the Far Eastern region meant these tank units were relegated to infantry support work.

Only in Manchuria did Japanese tank units come into their own.

In Russia, tank production outstripped all the rest of the world during the 1930s. Stalin, authorized the formation of two mechanized corps in 1933. Marshal Mikhail Tukhachevskii envisaged massive tank armies and by 1935 he had some 10,000 tanks under his command. This was a tremendous effort considering that only five years earlier the Soviet Union only possessed 30 tanks. Advances in tank warfare continued to be revolutionary in nature in Russia until 1937, when Tukhachevskii and many of the country's leading armored officers were executed in Stalin's purges. This culling of the brightest and best of the Red Army's tank officers severely curtailed Soviet armored developments and led to many tanks being transferred from independent mechanized corps to infantry support roles during the last years of the 1930s.

Germany's interest in tanks blossomed in the early 1920s as the lessons of World War I were absorbed. One of the benefits of the downsizing of the *Reichswehr* in the post-Versailles era was that many of the older more conservative officers opposed to tanks were retired, allowing younger more forward-looking officers to take over the future development of the Germany military.

The *Reichswehr's* secret links with the Soviet Union allowed for the testing of prototype German tanks in the depths of Russia, away from the prying eyes of British and French intelligence. Offensive operations were central to German thinking on tank warfare. Tanks were to be combined with the infiltration or stormtrooper tactics that had proved so successful at spreading confusion in the ranks of the Allied armies in 1917–18.

German tank enthusiasts, such as Heinz Guderian, were convinced that tanks must be used *en masse* to create maximum shock impact among the enemy. They also believed that German tanks had to have better firepower and armor than any enemy tank they might encounter on the battlefield. Guderian was very impressed by the British experiments and put particular emphasis on ensuring that every tank and vehicle in the German armored formations, the famous Panzer divisions, was equipped with radios to allow it to fight in a fast moving and highly flexible way.

What made the German approach to tank warfare fundamentally different from the British and French was their combination of tanks into specialist divisions, which combined tanks, with self-propelled guns, motorized infantry, engineers and logistic support. These

Right: **Panzer Is are put through their paces at a theatrical Nazi party rally in the late 1930s. These events served to demonstrate the power of the new Germany, although they had little military utility.**

Top right: **Panzer IIs spearheaded the German occupations of the Rhineland, Austria and Czechoslovakia, which convinced Hitler that Britain and France had no stomach to resist his territorial ambitions in Eastern Europe.**

Far right: **Senior Nazi party leaders took a close interest in the development of Germany's tank forces.**

divisions were intended to be used for strategic operations, pushing deep behind enemy lines to inflict decisive defeats.

Thanks to Hitler's enthusiastic support for the Panzer divisions, the German Army created a strategic armored force which was designed to deliver a knockout blow against Germany's enemies. Hitler was gambling the future of his Third Reich on *Blitzkrieg* war. His opponents were still largely thinking of refighting World War I.

Tank Technology

The end of World War I significantly reduced interest in new tank designs among the major powers. Several designs in Britain, France, Germany and the United States that were near production were simply scrapped. There was a massive scaling back in government funding for military production. Any innovative ideas and designs for new tanks were left in the hands of a few enthusiastic army officers such as Martel, private individuals like Sir John Carden or J. Walter Christie, and armaments companies such as Vickers-Armstrong.

The main lessons of World War I for the future of the tank were that they needed to be faster and to have rotating turrets containing their main armament.

Improvements in tank engines, suspensions, transmissions and track configurations went hand-in-hand with advances in the civilian automotive industry during the 1920s. New track and suspension systems were designed that allowed tanks to reach speeds in excess of 30mph, an unheard of feat to World War I tankmen.

Name: **Combat Car T4E1**

Designer/Manufacturer:
U.S. Ordnance Department

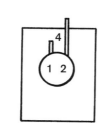

Weight: **8.9/10 tons
(9.1 tonnes)**

Main armament:
6 x machine guns

Hull length: **16ft 1in (4.9m)**

Width: **7ft 7in (2.31m)**

Height: **6ft 6in (1.98m)**

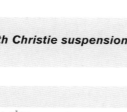

Speed: **25mph (40km/hr)**

Crew: **3**

Date entered service:
1933

Claim to fame:
**Typical experimental tank with Christie suspension
system**

Name:
Vickers Medium Mark I

Designer/Manufacturer:
Vickers-Armstrong

Weight: **11.7/13.1 tons
(11.9 tonnes)**

Main armament: **1 x 3-pdr (47mm)**

Secondary armament: **6 x machine guns**

Powerplant: **90hp Armstrong-Siddeley gasoline**

Frontal armor: **6.5mm**

Hull length: **17ft 6in
(5.33m)**

Width: **9ft 2in (2.79m)**

Height: **9ft 3in (2.82m)**

Speed: **15mph (24km/hr)**

Crew: **6**

Date entered service:
1924

Claim to fame: **First tank with three-man turret**

In the United States, the inventor and entrepreneur J. Walter Christie designed a revolutionary tank with a big-wheel suspension system which ultimately proved the inspiration for several generations of Soviet tank designs, beginning with the BT fast tank series, and extending to the war-winning T-34 and post-war T-55/62 family of tanks. Christie's early tanks also featured sloped armor, which had very impressive protective qualities. Britain also adopted Christie's suspension design as the basis for its series of cruiser tanks which ultimately led to the post-war Centurion.

Perhaps the most influential tank design of the inter-war period was the so-called Vickers Medium, which the British started to build in 1923. It was the first tank to enter service that featured a rotating three-man

Left: The T5 Combat Car was the forefather of the M3 (Light) Stuart, M3 (Medium) Lee and M4 Sherman tanks which were the mainstays of the U.S. Army's tank fleet during World War II.

Below left: A Vickers Medium Mark 2 of the Royal Tank Corps during the famous Mechanized Force experimental maneuvers. These tanks were best sellers around the world during the inter-war period.

Below right: A Panzer I shows its ability to drive through walls. In reality the vehicle was poorly armored and armed and proved highly vulnerable to anti-tank gun fire during the Spanish Civil War.

turret containing its main armament. This configuration would soon became almost standard for tanks around the world. Its 3-pounder (47mm) main armament was able to penetrate the armor of any tank then in existence. No longer were tanks mere infantry support weapons, now they could hunt down and destroy the enemy's armor. The turret also meant the commander was able to get a good view of the battlefield for the first time, allowing him to select targets for the gunner and navigate the vehicle. The fitting of radio sets in the late 1920s gave the Vickers Medium all the features that are now taken as standard on tanks.

The vehicle's top speed of 15mph and 150-mile radius of action meant it now had strategic reach beyond the small area of battlefield close to its base

camp. New gear and clutch arrangements made steering relatively easy. Major improvements were also made to the reliability of the vehicle's engine and running gear, making it possible for tank commanders to have confidence that their vehicles could be used for extended periods of time.

Britain's meager defense budget during the 1920s and 1930s also led to attempts to develop cheaper vehicles. These produced a series of two-man light tanks, or tankettes, made by both Vickers-Armstrong and Carden-Loyd. These vehicles were exported in large numbers to Russia, Italy and Japan and were the basis for many of these countries' designs during World War II.

Once rearmament was declared in the 1930s, the German tank industry swung into high gear with a series of designs that were to serve as the basis for bulk of their Panzer fleet until 1945. Central to German thinking on tank design was the need to equip their vehicles with as powerful an armament as possible. The Germans also recognized early on that it might be necessary in the future to up-gun their tanks, so each design was developed with future growth in mind. This was particularly important in terms of the size of the turret ring, which determined the size of the main armament that could be carried. The famous Panzer IV first entered production in 1937 and was still being produced as the Russians entered Berlin eight years later, after being upgraded no less than ten times. The Panzer IV, and its little brother the Panzer III, boasted many features that soon became standard on tanks, such as powered turret traverse and turret cupolas to give commanders a 360-degree view of the battlefield.

Tank armament also underwent considerable advances during the 1920s and 1930s. Most tanks,

---

Name: Panzer I Ausführung A

Designer/Manufacturer: Krupps and others

Weight: 5.3/5.9 tons (5.4 tonnes)

Main armament: 2 x machine guns

Powerplant: 57hp gasoline

Hull length: 13ft 2in (4.02m)

Width: 6ft 9in (2.06m)

Height: 5ft 8in (1.72m)

Speed: 23mph (37km/hr)

Crew: 2

Date entered service: 1935

Claim to fame: First Wehrmacht tank after Hitler ordered rearmament

Anti-tank mines had been used to some success during World War I and many nations continued to develop them. They employed simple weight-sensitive fuses to trigger them. The damage was usually not enough to destroy a tank but they could be guaranteed to blow off a track, resulting in immobilization. Once static a tank became very vulnerable to anti-tank gunners.

The 1920s and 1930s also saw the development of families of vehicles to support the tanks in the new armored divisions being fielded by many nations. The British generally relied on fleets of carriers developed from the Carden-Loyd tankettes for carrying infantry, machine-gun and anti-tank rifle teams, as well as reconnaissance tasks, while the Germans and Americans designed armored half tracks to do many of these tasks. The Germans and Russians were also great believers in self-propelled artillery.

Experience of Battle

During World War I the experience of combat was a great spur to technological development but in the largely peaceful 1920s and 1930s such a help to innovation was lacking. This was largely responsible for much of the muddled thinking about tank warfare in the years immediately before World War II.

The one major European conflict in the 1930s, the Spanish Civil War, saw a number of small scale tank engagements that led to many false lessons being drawn. Soviet BT tanks were supplied to the Republican side, along with "advisors" to operate them, by Stalin. Likewise Hitler and Mussolini sent tanks to help the Fascists. Spain's mountainous geography and a lack of logistic support facilities, however, meant that neither side was able to concentrate large tank forces for major attacks. Only a handful of tanks ever met on the battlefield. The results were inconclusive and seemed to indicate that well-sited and handled anti-tank guns could neutralize any tank threat.

On the far side of the world, a more significant experiment in tank warfare went largely unnoticed elsewhere. In response to a Japanese border incursion in May 1939 into Mongolia from Manchuria, the Russians under the command of the little known General Georgi Zhukov, massed almost 500 tanks and 100,000 men to evict the 75,000-strong Japanese force that included some 200 tanks. Unlike the Japanese, who spread their tanks out among their infantry, Zhukov grouped his armor into mobile strike forces. On 20th August Zhukov struck. An artillery barrage first silenced Japanese air defense artillery to open the way for Soviet bombers to roam over the battlefield

except for reasons best known to themselves, British infantry tanks, were equipped with specialist armor-piercing rounds made of hardened steel and shaped with an ogival nose literally to punch through tank armor because of the kinetic energy provided by the round's propellant charge.

At the same time as tank designs were evolving, the development of anti-tank guns also continued. High velocity anti-tank guns were produced by most of the major powers to provide protection for their infantry units. Weapons such as the British 2-pounder or German and Russian 37mm were built in large numbers. Taking the experience of World War I German armor-piercing machine-gun bullets one stage further, many countries also developed specialist anti-tank rifles that could be carrier and used by individual infantrymen. These had long barrels to enhance their velocity and hence hitting power, as well as hardened steel or tungsten-cored projectiles.

Again as a result of their wartime experience, the Germans put considerable effort into providing their anti-tank guns with self-propelled carriers to ensure they could be concentrated rapidly in threatened sectors of the front. The Germans also remembered to provide their new 88mm anti-aircraft or Flak gun with armor-piercing rounds, so they could be pressed into service as emergency anti-tank weapons.

destroying Japanese artillery batteries. Then Soviet artillery started to pound the Japanese infantry positions. Now Zhukov unleashed his armored reserves, which burst through the stunned Japanese infantry units. Soviet infantry rode into the battle on the backs of Zhukov's tanks. The Soviet tank forces did not stop to mop-up the remains of the frontline positions but just kept driving for 20 miles until two Japanese divisions were surrounded. Follow-up Soviet infantry divisions spent several days clearing out the remains of the Japanese frontline positions, while Zhukov positioned his tanks to deal with any counterattack.

The Japanese tried to intervene with their sole tank regiment, but Soviet bombers spotted it moving across the steppe and stopped it in its tracks. After a week, the Japanese threw in the towel after losing some 40,000 men. They signed a humiliating treaty recognising the Mongolian border on 15th September in Moscow. The Japanese had been the victims of the first ever *Blitzkrieg* attack but the U.S. and the major western European powers took little notice of the events on the Mongolian steppe—they were preoccupied with the looming war with Germany.

Left: **Cleaning the main armament of a Vickers Medium tank. This proved a reliable and effective tank during the inter-war period.**

Below: **Vickers Medium tanks are prepared for the British Army's famous Mechanized Force experimental maneuvers that did so much to prove that tanks could transform warfare.**

The Battlefield

World War II was the conflict that really put the tank on the map as a weapon of war. The tank rapidly matured technologically under the pressure of global war and almost every army recast its tactics and doctrine to bring tanks to the fore. Tanks, along with the widespread use of aircraft, meant that World War II would be a war of maneuver rather than a repeat of the stalemate that characterized World War I.

There was also a dramatic transformation of the nature of warfare due to a combination of factors—the ideological nature of war, the sheer number of participants in the conflict, as well as technological and industrial developments. In 1914, Europe's governments stumbled into war almost by accident. European societies went to war enthusiastically. This was an anachronistic conflict called by governments and monarchies for esoteric geopolitical reasons rather than a war for national survival. It was with great reluctance that moves had been made to mobilize Europe's societies for total conflict in the final years of the war.

The World War II was fundamentally different. Nazi Germany, Soviet Russia and the Japanese Empire whipped their populations into a fanatical frenzy of hate against their enemies. Their war aim was to eradicate their opponents from the face of the planet, or at least that part of it which they wished to rule. Whole countries were to be occupied, governments overthrown and populations deported or exterminated. Once the nature of this war dawned on the British and later the American people, they reacted in kind and developed strategies to defeat and occupy the Axis nations. This was total war. Every human, military, technological and industrial resource was mobilized for the war effort to achieve total victory.

At the peak of the war the United States and USSR each mobilized more than 12 million men and the British Empire put 8 million men into the field, while Germany mobilized almost 11 million troops and Japan

raised 6 million men. This was more than double the number of men mobilized during World War I. By the end of the war some 55 million people had died, several times the total toll in the 1914–18 conflict.

World War II spread to every continent of the globe. With maneuver returned to the battlefield by the mechanization of armies, it was possible to advance rapidly across huge distances in a way that had not been possible before. France fell to the German *Blitzkrieg* in a matter of weeks and it only took Hitler's armies five months to get from Poland to the suburbs of Moscow.

Left, Above, and Over page: **The Blitzkrieg rolls. German tanks move forward during the dramatic dash for the English Channel that completely confounded the British and French in May 1940.**

To prevail on this new mechanized battlefield required technological and industrial supremacy. The war was waged not just on the battlefronts but in laboratories, design studios and factories. The nation that developed and fielded better tanks, planes, ships, guns and submarines would have a war winning advantage. The fate of nations turned on their ability to manage this process better than their opponents.

On the battlefield this meant that armies had to be constantly deploying new weapons and developing new ways of using them to give them a decisive advantage over their enemies. Armies that embraced new ideas were able to win stunning victories, while those that chose to rest on their laurels doomed their nations to defeat and occupation. A new generation of professional soldiers, sailors and airmen emerged who were comfortable with machines and not afraid to discard old ideas and "think out of the box." These men soon came to dominate the armies of the world, consigning forever the amateur gentleman soldiers of the 19th century to the dustbin of history.

The struggles of tank enthusiasts during the inter-war years to get their armies to move towards mechanized warfare epitomized what was involved in moving military science forward. The success of the German *Blitzkrieg* in 1939–40 was a major wake-up call for the opponents of Hitler. All around Europe the German Panzer divisions swept away the old military order that had been on life-support after World War I. In America, Britain, and Russia there was a realization that unless they also adopted the German style of warfare there would be no hope of defeating Hitler's ambitions.

Land warfare changed forever when the first German tanks crossed the border into Poland on September 1, 1939. The German Army not only employed tanks *en masse*, but it was a thoroughly modern and forward-looking organization, that had been indoctrinated with a will to win lacking elsewhere in Europe at the time.

German units were equipped with large numbers of modern and efficient radios that enabled tank, artillery and air attacks to be rapidly co-ordinated. Logistic support of the tank spearheads was based on motorized truck convoys, though most of the German Army still relied on railroads and horse-drawn transport. German battlefield commanders were delegated authority to

make tactical decisions without reference to rear headquarters. The Germans had correctly learned the lessons from the British experience of World War I. It was not enough just to have good modern tanks; they had to be integrated into a whole system of warfare that could capitalize on their initial successes against the enemy frontline. Once the tanks had broken through the enemy front, the Panzer divisions had to have the mobility, logistic support and communications to enable them to turn a tactical advantage into strategic exploitation.

In 1939 and 1940 the Poles, British and French possessed more tanks and men than the Germans but they were unable to comprehend that their systems of making war were obsolete. The Germans were able rapidly to turn local success into a series of crushing victories, culminating in the defeat of France in June 1940. Yet, within two years, the German Panzer force was itself in relative decline due to the Herculean efforts of the British, Russians and, later, Americans to catch up. Ultimately the very sophistication of German tanks proved a crucial failing, because the Third Reich was simply not able to mass-produce tanks on the scale achieved by its opponents.

The extent of the disparity between German tank production levels and those of its enemies can be gauged from the fact that America built some 88,000 tanks in World War II, Russia 93,000, Britain 24,800 and Germany only 24,350. Despite German tanks such as the Tiger and Panther being technologically superior to their rivals, their kill rate was nowhere near enough to allow Hitler's troops to gain a decisive battlefield advantage. In 1943 the Germans knocked out 23,000 Soviet tanks, but the Soviets just built 29,000 more in the following year.

Compared to World War I, tank crews had to fight on a very different battlefield. Tanks were now considered battle-winning weapons and they were usually at the center of a commander's tactical plans. The tanks of themselves were far more mechanically mature and reliable. They had evolved into complex weapon systems, which the crews had to master fully if they were to survive on the battlefield.

This in turn meant that the pace and tempo of battle was dramatically different. Tank units could move

Above: **France's Somua 35S was more than a match for the German tanks of the late 1930s but was never available in large enough numbers to make an impact on the fighting in May 1940.**

Far left: **The 1st Panzer Division moves into Poland in September 1939 to spearhead Hitler's first Blitzkrieg victory.**

Left: **A Char B1 abandoned during the rout of 1940, when the French proved no match for the more mobile and dynamic German Panzer divisions.**

rapidly over large distances to engage an enemy. Once in battle, they received their orders over radios and often fought as part of large formations. Tank crews had to work hand-in-hand with their comrades to defeat the enemy by maneuver, surprise and guile. Only by successfully co-ordinating tanks with infantry, artillery and air support could well armed and trained opponents be overcome.

For the individual tank crew the terror of combat was little different from that experienced by their predecessors in World War I. The view of the battlefield through narrow vision ports from inside tanks was still limited. Mines still blew off tracks, armor-piercing shells ripped through even the thickest armor and a lingering horrible death was a near certainty if crews were trapped inside a burning tank.

However, the continuous fielding of new and improved tanks, with better armor, guns and engines, meant that for fleeting periods of the war some tank crews were provided with vehicles superior to their opponents. The crews of the first German Tigers or the later Soviet Josef Stalin II heavy tanks were almost invulnerable to any enemy anti-tank weapons. They could sweep all before them and remain impervious. They were masters of the battlefield—a tank commander's dream.

Tank warfare evolved rapidly as the war went on, with new battlefronts opening and new designs being fielded. For almost two years the German Panzer divisions reigned supreme as they capitalized on the advantages gained during Hitler's rearmament campaign. Polish, British and French tank forces were shattered in battle. In the North African desert during

1941 British armored units were at first victorious against poorly led and motivated Italian forces. The intervention of the German *Afrika Korps* under Erwin Rommel turned the tide against the British Eighth Army. For two years a see-saw battle raged along the North African coast as the British and Germans each fielded new tanks to gain superiority over their enemy.

The June 1941 invasion of Russia began a truly titanic struggle between Hitler's Panzers and Stalin's tank armies. In spite of losing more than 10,000 tanks in the first months of Operation Barbarossa, the Russians relocated their tank factories to east of the Ural mountains and began churning out tens of thousands of war-winning T-34s. By the summer of 1943 the Red Army had regained the initiative from the *Wehrmacht* and began a relentless advance into the heart of the Third Reich.

U.S. troops first fought the Germans in Northwest Africa in late 1942. By then the M4 Sherman was already in production as the standard American battle tank. Hard lessons were learned in combat, especially during the Battle of Kasserine in February 1943. After sweeping the Germans out of North Africa in May 1943, combined British and American forces invaded Sicily and later the Italian mainland. Fierce fighting followed as veteran German units mounted a deliberate withdrawal up the Italian peninsula but the rugged and mountainous terrain meant tanks were never able to come to the fore during the bloody Italian campaign.

The invasion of Normandy by American and Allied troops in June 1944 pitted the élite of Hitler's Panzer force against some 8,000 allied tanks. The German defenders were eventually overwhelmed by the weight

Left: **"The T-34 always raises its hat to a Tiger"** was a German saying on the Eastern Front. Earlier versions of the mass-produced Soviet tank were out-gunned by the German Tigers and Panthers from 1943 onwards until up-gunned T-34/85s were available.

Above right: **A Cromwell tank of the British 7th Armoured Division speeds across the French countryside in August 1944, as the Allies began their pursuit of the defeated German Army.**

of the Allied attack and soon Lieutenant General George Patton's Third Army was racing across France to the border of the Third Reich in one of the most dramatic advances in the history of armored warfare. Hitler mustered his last reserve in December 1944 to strike back against the allies in the Battle of the Bulge but the Panzer attack was soon halted. Over the next five months British and American attacks in the west and Russian offensives from the east crushed the remains of the *Wehrmacht* and in the last days of April 1945 Soviet tanks stormed into Berlin to end the war in Europe.

Japanese attacks in the Far East from December 1941 swept American, British and Dutch forces before them. Jungle warfare did not lend itself to mass armored battles or maneuvers but small numbers of Japanese tanks played a key role in their offensive strategy, spreading confusion and fear among the poorly trained and motivated allied garrisons in the Philippines, Malaysia, the Dutch East Indies and Burma. In jungle warfare and amphibious operations later in the war the Allied tanks were always used in infantry support roles. The only massed used of tanks in the war against Japan occurred in August 1945, when a huge force of 5,500 Russian tanks was unleashed against Manchuria, defeating more than a million Japanese soldiers.

Tactical and Doctrinal Development

German Panzer divisions transformed armored tactics because they placed tanks at the forefront of the action, rather than relegating them to supporting the infantry.

The Germans formed their own Panzer branch on a par with the infantry and artillery to ensure that their new armored force was never shackled by the requirements of the other arms of service. This was further enhanced by that fact that experienced tank officers were always placed in command of Panzer divisions.

The Panzer divisions were built around a tank component of at least regimental/brigade strength, teamed with a full complement of supporting infantry, artillery, air defense guns, anti-tank guns, engineers, reconnaissance troops, communications and logistic units. These units were tailored to support the division's tanks in both defense and attack. Combined arms battlegroups, or *Kampfgruppen*, were the norm in Panzer divisions so specialist troops could be placed under tank commanders for particular missions. Radios fitted to each German tank or armored vehicle in the Panzer divisions meant that their commanders could control forces over long distances and execute complex tactical maneuvers. German tank crews were also able to carry out complex fire control procedures for the first time in tank warfare because of their extensive radio communications nets. This also allowed them to put into practice fire-and-maneuver tactics, providing covering fire for other tanks as they crossed open ground or obstacles.

German tank tactics emphasized using tanks *en masse*, generally at least in battalion or regimental strength both in attack or defense. The legacy of the World War I infiltration or stormtrooper tactics was rapidly assimilated by German Panzer commanders. In the attack, Panzer commanders tried to avoid wasting away their tanks with direct assaults on enemy positions. Where possible, they unleashed their tanks in strength against weak points in the enemy front. Employ your strength against the enemy's weakness was the watchword of the Panzer crews. Once a breakthrough was achieved, the Germans then reinforced success and pushed in reserves to capitalize on it. After breaking through, the Panzer divisions would push deep behind enemy lines, attacking supply dumps, artillery positions and headquarters rather than worrying about rounding up by-passed infantry.

PHASE 1

Left and below left: German tank formations–the *Kolonne*, or column, was used for assembly; the *Keil* was an attack formation for a narrow front; the *Breitkeil*, as the name implies, was for a broader front. The lower formation is another battalion attacking formation.

Far right: **An M10 Tank Destroyer on the prowl. Armed with a 75mm gun it was the U.S. Army's principal anti-tank weapon during World War II.**

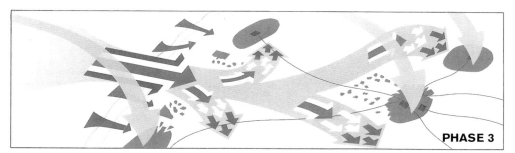

PHASE 2

Left: **The stages of *Blitzkrieg*. Phase 1, use of airpower and concentration of armored thrust. Phase 2, the push begins. Phase 3, bypassing troop concentrations, the *Blitzkrieg* juggernaut rolls on. Bypassed concentrations are encircled and squeezed. Phase 4, the success is exploited.**

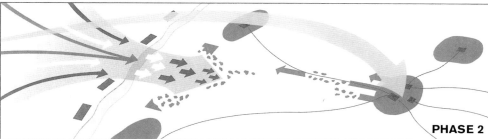

PHASE 3

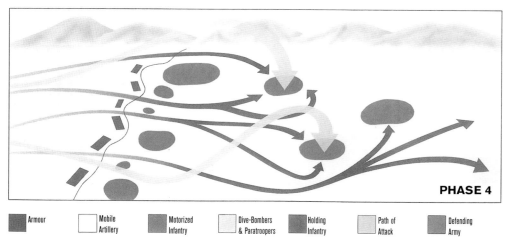

PHASE 4

| Armour | Mobile Artillery | Motorized Infantry | Dive-Bombers & Paratroopers | Holding Infantry | Path of Attack | Defending Army |

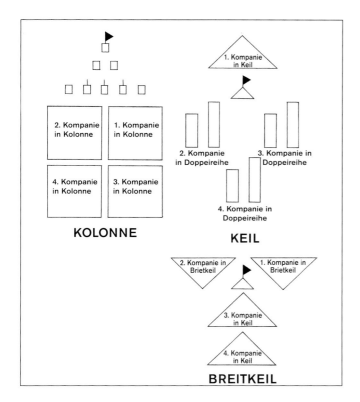

KOLONNE

2. Kompanie in Kolonne | 1. Kompanie in Kolonne
4. Kompanie in Kolonne | 3. Kompanie in Kolonne

KEIL

1. Kompanie in Keil
2. Kompanie in Doppeireihe | 3. Kompanie in Doppeireihe
4. Kompanie in Doppeireihe

BREITKEIL

2. Kompanie in Brietkeil | 1. Kompanie in Brietkeil
3. Kompanie in Keil
4. Kompanie in Keil

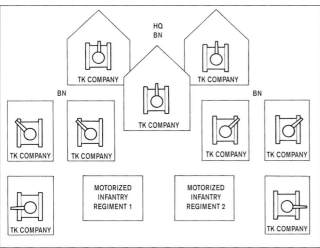

Tank units advanced in a flexible formation called the Panzer wedge, with the most heavily armored and armed tanks, such as Panthers or Tigers, in the van. It was their job to take on and destroy enemy anti-tank guns. Riding in the wake of the heavy Panzers were lighter tanks, anti-tank guns and motorized infantry (Panzergrenadiers) in half tracks. If any enemy tanks tried to counterattack, the anti-tank guns would deploy to shield the Panzers to allow them to continue their advance uninterrupted.

In defense the Panzer divisions also tried to employ their tanks as hard-hitting counterattack forces, rather than scatter them in penny packets among frontline infantry units. The fielding of the Panther and Tiger tanks during 1942–43 meant that German tanks in the final years of the war possessed firepower and armored protection superior to most of their opponents. This meant they were able to engage their targets from long ranges and remain invulnerable to most Allied weapons.

After years of neglect and internal rivalry in the 1920s and 1930s, the U.S. Army reacted quickly to the success of the German Panzer divisions in 1939 and 1940. The formation of the Armored Force in 1940, later the Armored Command, was quickly followed by the creation of the first armored divisions. Within two years there were 16 U.S. armored divisions. U.S. armored divisions followed closely the model of the Panzer divisions, with a good balance of armor, infantry, artillery, engineering, logistic and reconnaissance units. Each division had three combat commands, which were flexible headquarters that could have a mix of units attached for a particular operation in the manner of the German *Kampfgruppen*.

American armored commanders, such as George Patton, had a strategic vision for their new divisions. Great emphasis was placed on rapid long-range movement and efficient logistic support, as well as air support for reconnaissance and attack. Tactics were developed to make decisive breakthroughs and then exploit deep behind enemy lines. Anti-tank help for the infantry was left to specially formed tank destroyer units, leaving armored units free for wide-ranging offensive operations.

In order to produce the largest possible tank force the U.S. Army initially chose to spurn heavy tanks in favor of large numbers of lighter and more maneuverable Sherman tanks. Over 40,000 Shermans were built in all. When first produced in 1942 it compared reasonably well with contemporary Panzer IV models but by 1944–45 it was totally outclassed. When they faced heavy German Panthers and Tigers, U.S. tank crews had to rely on artillery fire support, air attacks and overwhelming numbers to overcome them. Complex maneuvers had to be undertaken to co-ordinate the movement of Shermans onto the flanks of German tanks to engage their weak side armor.

During the breakout from Normandy the U.S. Third Army was able to advance at a phenomenal rate, by-passing German resistance and striking out almost unopposed to the German border. Patton's rapid response to the German Ardennes offensive in December 1944 also demonstrated that U.S. armored divisions were capable of nimble battlefield maneuvers that completely confounded the Germans and compensated in part for the tactical shortcomings of the U.S. Army's tanks.

The U.S. Marine Corps fielded large numbers of Sherman tanks and Landing Vehicles Tracked (LTVs) during its island-hopping campaign in the Pacific, to provide mobile firepower and armored protection. Tanks and LTVs were crucial during the first hours of amphibious landings to neutralize Japanese machine-gun nests and protect Marines pinned down on open beaches.

If the German Panzer divisions were the revolutionary visionaries of warfare, the Red Army was the nemesis of Hitler armored warriors. After being thoroughly thrashed in the months after the German invasion of Russia in 1941, the Red Army's armored force began a long road to recovery. Stalin's generals recognized that they were never going to be able to replicate the sophisticated Panzer units of the *Wehrmacht*, so they opted to overwhelm the Germans with massive numbers of tanks. They first created tank corps of around 200 tanks, and then combined several

Right: **The remains of an A9 cruiser tank of the British 1st Armoured Division. The unit was almost completely destroyed in France in 1940.**

Below right: **The different types of minefield laid in front of an advancing enemy. Red indicates anti-personnel and blue anti-tank mines. First, a "nuisance" field slows the initial advance. Next a barrier field at a road junction channels enemy units into a killing zone. Phoney–marked but unsown–fields push the enemy into thicker minefields near defensive positions, around which anti-tank minefields will hinder enemy movements when the positions are overrun.**

Below: **Abandoned Panzer IVs littered Russia in 1943 and 1944 as the Red Army's tank armada developed into an unstoppable torrent.**

of these into tank armies. Red Army tank corps contained a small number of submachine-gun armed infantry to ride into action on the tanks. Their job was to keep German anti-tank rocket teams at bay and prevent the advance stalling.

It was rare for a tank corps to be committed to action by itself. Usually several divisions worth of artillery and multi-barrel rocket launchers were concentrated along the section of German front to be attacked. Their barrage was usually enough literally to obliterate any German positions barring the advance. The tank corps then just drove forward, rolling over the remains of the frontline and pushing deep into the German rear area. If the Germans managed to muster a Panzer counterattack force, then the tank corps would be turned to face the threat and take on the Panzers.

Russian tank tactics were crude. Only battalion and company commanders had radios, so once a tank corps was committed to action it was not unusual for senior officers to lose control of events totally. Tank crews had to be given very specific geographic objectives otherwise they tended to get hopelessly lost because only senior officers had maps. Tank-to-tank engagements became very confused on the Soviet side, because the lack of radios that mean no coherent fire control mechanisms existed. Soviet tank tactics rarely got beyond wild charges towards the enemy for this reason. These may have been unsophisticated but

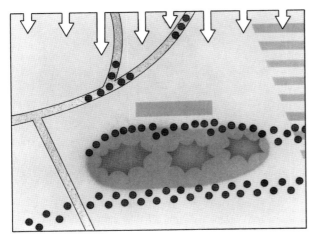

Soviet tank corps and armies were awesome weapons of war. They rarely failed to sweep all before them.

While Soviet tank forces lacked the polish of their German counterparts, the Red Army anti-tank gunners proved to be very skilful and determined opponents. Bitter experience taught the Soviets that, if they allowed the Germans to maneuver on a battlefield, they would be lost. Soviet anti-tank defenses were therefore

perfected to a high degree and specialist anti-tank brigades formed. Scores of 76.2mm high velocity anti-tank guns were emplaced in reinforced bunkers with overlapping arcs of fire so all the guns of a brigade could concentrate their fire on a single German tank. In front of the brigade, hundreds of anti-tank mines would be sewn to force the Germans to stall their attack to allow engineers to come forward to clear lanes in the minefield. Halted tanks were far easier targets. After they suffered heavy losses to Soviet anti-tank gunners during the Battle of Kursk the German tank crews began to fear these positions and dubbed them "*Pakfronts*." Their destruction was usually left to heavily armored Tigers and Panthers, with other elements of the Panzer divisions keeping out of their way.

After pioneering tank warfare in World War I, Britain's efforts to take on the German Panzers were hampered by muddled thinking at the top of the War Office that worked its way through into the poor designs of tanks. The huge losses in France in 1940 further put back Britain's effort to build a counter-weight to the Panzers. The decision taken in the late 1930s to divide Britain's tank force into "infantry," "cruiser" and "light" units was the root of the problem. The heavily armored infantry tanks were allocated to work with infantry units, leaving the faster but less well armed and armored cruiser tanks to take on enemy armor. This artificial division of tank types meant cruiser tanks had no high explosive ammunition to engage infantry targets or anti-tank guns, only armor-piercing, while the first infantry tanks relied on machine guns to engage enemy infantry and had no heavier weapons. The light tanks carried out only scouting and screening tasks. An armored division equipped almost exclusively with cruiser tanks was formed and sent to France in 1940 where it was destroyed. British armored divisions were far too top heavy with tanks, with few infantry and artillery units to provide vital support and making them difficult to maneuver. Armor-infantry co-operation was always a problem below brigade level, with infantry companies rarely being attached to tank regiments leaving the tanks vulnerable to German anti-tank guns. The British were slow to field armored personnel carriers or half

tracks so it was always difficult for infantry to keep up with tank advances.

The Eighth Army's duels with the *Afrika Korps* provided further confirmation that the British Royal Armoured Corps was outclassed by the Panzers. British armor was regularly divided up between brigade groups that could be easily isolated and destroyed in detail by Rommel's Panzers. Generally Rommel simply drew British tanks onto his 88mm Flak guns and 50mm anti-tank guns, which inflicted more losses on the British tanks than the German tanks did.

The technical inferiority of the Eighth Army's Crusader, Matilda II, and Valentine tanks to the Panzer

German tanks

British tanks

Burned-out British tanks

British mine-clearers

British infantry and 6 pounder anti-tank guns

British tanks attacking

German 50mm gun

German 88mm gun

Minefield

British 25-pounder shell bursts on German positions

Right: **A German 88mm Flak gun and a StuG III assault gun await a Soviet tank assault. The 88 proved to be one of the best anti-tank guns of the war**

Left: **A typical desert engagement. Allied armor has broken through a minefield and is about to attack the enemy while a second path through the minefield is cleared and infantry support is coming forward. The German defensive position is being shelled in preparation for the attack. The defense is in layers: first the shorter-range 50mm anti-tank weapons; next, the powerful 88mm guns; finally, the Axis armor is held in reserve to plug gaps in the defense or counterattack as necessary.**

Below right: **German Panzer III tanks first saw service in Poland in 1939 and went on to be the mainstay of the Panzer force until late in 1942.**

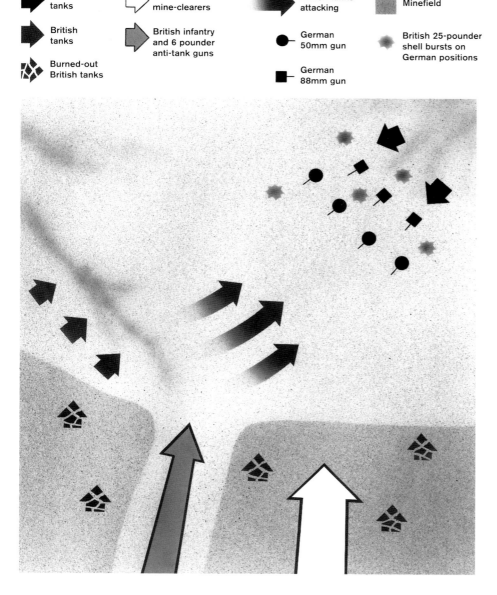

IIIs and IVs of the *Afrika Korps* meant that British tank crews were rarely able to fight the Germans on equal terms, creating a vicious circle of defeat, poor morale and retreat. The arrival of American-made General Grant (M3 Lee in U.S. service) and Sherman (M4) tanks in North Africa during 1942 redressed the North Africa armor balance, until the appearance of the Tiger in Tunisia in 1943.

The next major challenge for the Royal Armoured Corps was how to force a bridgehead on Hitler's Fortress Europe. The experience of the Dieppe raid in 1942 when Canadian-manned Churchill tanks had been unable to get off the beaches because of German fortifications and obstacles, led to the creation of the famous 79th Armoured Division, the so-called "Hobart's Funnies," with its menagerie of specialist combat engineering tanks. These included flame throwing tanks called Crocodiles, swimming Sherman tanks (or DDs, standing for Duplex Drive), bridging tanks called Arcs, mine-clearing tanks called Flails or Crabs and engineering tanks with heavy petard mortars to blast away pill boxes or concrete obstacles. These tanks ensured the British Army was able to establish itself ashore on D-Day with light casualties. U.S. leaders decided not to adopt most of these variants, however, a decision which contributed to the heavy casualty toll suffered on Omaha Beach.

Once ashore in Normandy British tank crews again found themselves at a disadvantage against the German Panthers and Tigers. British tank units were only able to fight these monsters with any reasonable chance of

success if they had the Firefly version of the Sherman tank armed with the high velocity 17-pounder gun. With other types of tank, like the standard version of the Sherman which was the most numerous tank in British service, it was almost impossible to take on the heavy German armor at long range, so the British tanks crews had to try to work their way around the flanks of their opponents to get off shots against their exposed flanks. This was an almost suicidal exercise.

The Royal Artillery was responsible for anti-tank defense in the British Army and, like its Soviet counterparts, it became a very efficient organization.

Left: **By up-gunning and up-armoring their tanks, such as this Panzer IIIJ, the Germans were able to react rapidly to new enemy technological developments.**

Right: **A column of Panzer IVFs of the *Grossdeutschland* Division rolls forward to counter the 1942 Russian winter offensive.**

British anti-tank gun units deployed with forward tank and infantry units to hunt German Panzers.

Tank Technology

During the 1920s and 1930s tank technology advanced at a snail's pace, but once World War II got underway with a vengeance in 1940 the development of new and better tank designs accelerated dramatically. The success of the German Panzers in the *Blitzkrieg* years demonstrated beyond doubt the pre-eminence of firepower in the tank design equation. Armored protection and mobility were both nudged into second and third place by the requirement to be able to destroy the most heavily armored enemy tanks. Rival tank designers in Britain, Germany, Russia and the United States became locked in a battle to field more powerfully armed, better armored and faster tanks. As new enemy tanks and anti-tank weapons appeared on the battlefield, so the tank designers were spurred to develop tanks that could counteract them.

As well as changes to the tanks themselves there were also improvements to the ammunition they carried. At the start of the war tanks were only provided with a very limited variety of anti-armor ammunition, all based on kinetic energy principles, which relied on accelerating a shell to a very high velocity so it could punch through

Name: *Panzer IVH*

Designer/Manufacturer: *Krupps and others*

Weight: 23.1/25.9 tons (23.5 tonnes)

Main armament: *1 x 75mm*

Secondary armament: *2 x machine guns*

Powerplant: *300hp Maybach gasoline*

Frontal armor: *80mm*

Hull length: *19ft 6in (5.95m)*

Width: *9ft 5in (2.88m)*

Height: *8ft 9in (2.68m)*

Speed: *24mph (40km/hr*

Crew: *5*

Date entered service: *1943*

Claim to fame: *Most numerous German tank of World War II*

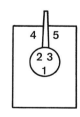

Name: Matilda II

Designer/Manufacturer: Vulcan Foundry and others

Weight: 26.5/29.7 tons (26.9 tonnes)

Main armament: 1 x 2-pdr (37mm)

Secondary armament: 1 x machine gun

Powerplant: 174hp diesel

Frontal armor: 78mm

Hull length: 18ft 5in (5.61m)

Width: 8ft 6in (2.59m)

Height: 8ft 3in (2.52m)

Speed: 15mph (25km/hr)

Crew: 4

Date entered service: 1938

Claim to fame: Most effective British tank of 1940–41 period

enemy armor. By the end of the war the selection had become much more sophisticated.

The British, French and Germans inevitably went into World War II with designs that were largely untested in combat. The battles in France in 1940 proved the first stimulus to innovation with the British and Germans taking away different lessons. The Germans were surprised by the heavy armor of the British and French tanks they encountered. Often the only weapons capable of penetrating the monster Char Bs and Matilda IIs were their 88mm Flak guns. Plans were put in place to up-gun the Panzer III fleet with 50mm high velocity cannon and, likewise, the Panzer IV was identified as a candidate for a long barrelled 75mm weapon. Both types were also up-armored after France.

The British saw at last the failure of their machine-gun armed Matilda I infantry tanks and directed attention to improving their cruiser tanks. Work was speeded up on the 6-pounder cannon to replace the obsolete 2-pounder, which was then the standard British tank main armament, although it was 1941 before this effective weapon was mounted in a tank.

In the United States, the appearance of the Panzer IV in 1939–40 led to the instigation of a crash program to install a 75mm cannon in a tank. This became known

Name: **M3 light Stuart**

Designer/Manufacturer: **American Car and Foundry**

Weight: **12.2/13.7 tons (12.4 tonnes)**

Main armament: **1 x 37mm**

Secondary armament: **5 x machine guns**

Powerplant: **250bhp Continental gasoline**

Armor: **37mm**

Hull length: **14ft 11in (4.54m)**

Width: **7ft 4in (2.23m)**

Height: **8ft 3in (2.51m)**

Speed: **36mph (57km/hr)**

Crew: **4**

Date entered service: **1940**

Claim to fame: **Standard U.S. light tank of WWII**

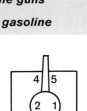

Name: **M4 medium Sherman**

Designer/Manufacturer: **Too many to note all**

Weight: **29.7/33.3 tons (30.2 tonnes)**

Main armament: **1 x 75mm**

Secondary armament: **3 x machine guns**

Powerplant: **500hp Ford gasoline (M4A3)**

Armor: **76mm**

Hull length: **19ft 4in (5.89m)**

Height: **9ft 0in (2.75m)**

Width: **8ft 7in (2.62m)**

Speed: **24mph (39km/hr)**

Crew: **5**

Date entered service: **1942**

Claim to fame: **Main U.S. tank of WWII**

as the M3 Lee (or Grant in British service). The 75mm gun was mounted in a hull sponson with only limited traverse but it was an important step forward. When transferred to British service from early 1942 it did much to redress the balance against the German Panzer IIIs and IVs in North Africa until the M4 Sherman became available to British forces later in that year.

The U.S. Army started a program to build a heavy tank early in the war, the T20, but this was cancelled before the D-Day landings in 1944 because of the problems of transporting them to overseas theaters of operation. Once the U.S. Army found itself up against German Panthers in Normandy, its Shermans, even the up-gunned versions with 76mm long cannons, were soon proved to be outclassed. The T10 designs were resurrected and the 90mm-armed M26 Pershing was born. Early examples were rushed to Europe in time for the invasion of Germany. Even though the tank was found to have many short comings, it became the basis for American tank designs of the immediate post-war period.

During the first two years of the war, the heavily armored British Matilda IIs were only checked by the German 88mm Flak guns. The British 2-pounder tank gun had little chance of penetrating the armor of the latest models of Panzer IIIs and IVs. In a bid to improve

Above: **The Allies landed some 8,000 tanks, the majority of them Shermans, in Northwest Europe as the fighting in Normandy reached its climax during June and July 1944.**

Far left: **U.S. Army Cavalry units carried out reconnaissance tasks ahead of armored units with the M3 Stuart light tank.**

Left: **The M3 Lee was the first Allied tank capable of taking on the German Panzer IIIs and IVs on equal terms thanks to its hull-mounted 75mm cannon.**

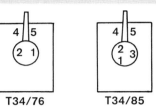

Name: *T-34/76 [T-34/85]*

Designer/Manufacturer:

Weight: *26.3/29.4 tons (26.7 tonnes) [31.5/35.3 tons (32 tonnes)]*

Main armament: *1 x 76mm [1 x 85mm]*

Secondary armament: *2 x machine guns*

Powerplant: *500hp, V-2-34 diesel*

Frontal armor: *45mm [75mm]*

Hull length: *20ft 3in (6.19m)*

Width: *9ft 7in (2.92m)*

Height: *7ft 10 in (2.39m) [9ft 0in (2.74m)]*

Speed: *31mph (50km/hr)*

Crew: *5*

Date entered service: *1940 [1943]*

Claim to fame: *First operational tank with sloped armor*

T34/76   T34/85

Above right: **The appearance of the T-34 in 1941 was a major surprise to the Germans and its superb performance during the Russian 1941 winter counteroffensive convinced the Germans they needed better tanks**

Right: **Until the appearance of the Tiger I in 1942, the heaviest German tank was the Panzer IV which was progressively up-gunned to meet new threats.**

Far right: **The German Panther tank borrowed the T-34's sloped armor and proved to be one of the best tank designs of the war**

Name: Panther D

Designer/Manufacturer: MAN, MNH, Henschel, DEMAG

Weight: 42.3/47.4 tons (43 tonnes)

Main armament: 75mm

Secondary armament: 2 x machine guns

Powerplant: 700hp Maybach gasoline

Frontal armor: 100mm

Hull length: 22ft 6in (6.85m)

Width: 11ft 2in (3.43m)

Height: 9ft 8in (2.97m)

Speed: 28mph (46km/hr)

Crew: 5

Date entered service: 1943

Claim to fame: Best all-round German tank of World War II

the performance of what was then their standard tank armament, the British fielded the armor-piercing/composite, non-rigid (AP/CNR) round which contained a hardened core of tungsten carbide, one of the hardest metals known to man. By using such materials it was possible to get better armor-piercing capabilities without having to increase the size of the gun. Normal armor-piercing rounds shatter if they hit metal at velocities beyond about 2,700 feet per second but tungsten-based ammunition could survive impacts at velocities up to 4,000 feet per second, dramatically improving its penetrating power. Another development was the fitting of hardened caps to kinetic energy rounds to prevent them breaking up on impact against hardened armor and so improving penetration. The British termed these as armor-piercing, capped, ballistic cap (APCBC) or armor-piercing cap (APC). Other nations followed a similar path of development and ammunition of these types was in widespread use by the middle years of the war.

The seminal event in the development of tank technology during World War II was the Germans' first

encounter with the Soviet T-34 in the summer of 1941. Literally overnight all the tanks in the *Wehrmacht* were obsolete and the Germans knew it. This, more than the tank duels in France or North Africa, stimulated a revolution in tank technology.

The T-34's sloped armor, powerful 76mm cannon, wide tracks for cross-country mobility and rugged reliability meant it was completely superior to the German tanks. It was virtually invulnerable to most German tank guns of the time—the short 75mm on Panzer IVs, and 50mm and 37mms on Panzer IIIs—while every German tank was easily penetrated by the T-34's gun. At first some German Panzer generals suggested that the T-34 should be built in Germany, but then two crash programs for new tanks were begun. As an interim measure to counter the T-34 the Germans issued AP/CR rounds to the 50mm-armed Panzer IIIs. Called the Panzergranate 40 (AP 40), shortage of tungsten meant this "silver bullet" could only be used very rarely; it was later made available for 75mm and 88mm guns.

Plans for a heavy tank were already on the drawing board in 1941 and these were quickly dusted off. This tank became known as the Tiger I and it remained a potent and feared weapon for the remainder of the war. Armed with an 88mm gun it could pick off all Allied tanks at ranges in excess of 1,500 yards, while its 100mm frontal armor made it impervious to any tank gun in Allied service when it was introduced in 1942. At the same time the Germans launched production of a new medium tank to replace the Panzer IV. The superlative Panther came into service in 1943 and boasted sloped armor like the T-34's, which offered the almost the same level of protection of the Tiger's armor but at a fraction of the weight. This meant the Panther was far more nimble than its big brother. Its long barrelled 75mm cannon gave the Panther far more reach and hitting power than the T-34/76, effectively restoring the German Army's qualitative tank superiority on the Eastern Front.

The appearance of the Tiger and then the Panther, created almost panic among British and Russian tank crews, commanders and designers. The British put their 17-pounder anti-tank gun into service in 1943 and provided it with the armor-piercing discarding sabot (APDS) round which could punch through a Panther's front armor at 1,500 yards. This wrapped a thin tungsten carbide sabot in a light casing that fell away after it was launched out of the gun barrel, considerably enhancing the projectile's velocity and penetrating power. The 17-pounder was then mounted in a Sherman to create the Firefly, the only British or American tank in 1944–45 able to fight the German Tigers or Panthers on anything like equal terms.

In Russia, the Red Army responded to the Tiger by dramatically improving the T-34. It was given extra armor, a new three-man turret with a commander's cupola to allow him better vision and an 85mm gun. The Soviets also upgraded their KV-series heavy tanks with 85mm guns. Then they fielded the Josef Stalin family of heavy tanks, which boasted heavier armor than the Tiger I, and a monster 122mm gun. With these tanks the Russian confirmed their armored supremacy on the Eastern Front in 1944. Only the appearance of the super-heavy Tiger II, which combined thick armor and an improved 88mm cannon with the Panther's sleek lines, gave the Germans some respite, but these were only produced in small numbers.

All sides in the war were looking for ways to improve the performance of their armor-piercing weapons without necessarily going down the road of increasing propellant and shell size, both of which necessitated increasing the size of the weapon and the vehicle to carry it, as they had in the super-heavy Tiger and Josef Stalin tanks. High explosive anti-tank (HEAT) weapons were

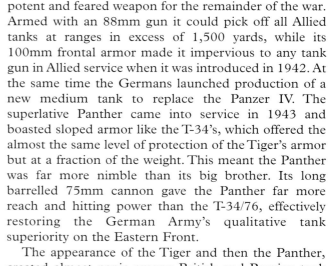

Name: Sherman Firefly

Designer/Manufacturer: Woolwich Arsenal

Weight: 32/35.8 tons (32.5 tonnes)

Main armament: 1 x 17-pdr (76mm)

Secondary armament: 1 x machine gun

Powerplant: 500hp Chrysler gasoline

Frontal armor: 76mm

Hull length: 19ft 4in (5.89m)

Width: 8ft 7in (2.62m)

Height: 9ft 0in (2.75m)

Speed: 24mph 39km/hr

Crew: 5

Date entered service: 1944

Claim to fame: Only Allied tank capable of fighting Tigers and Panthers on near equal terms

Name: Tiger II

Designer/Manufacturer: Henschel

Weight: 68.3/76.5 tons (69.4 tonnes)

Main armament: 1 x 88mm

Secondary armament: 2 x machine guns

Powerplant: 700hp Maybach gasoline

Frontal armor: 180mm

Hull length: 23ft 9in (7.23m)

Width: 12ft 3in (3.73m)

Height: 10ft 1in (3.08m)

Speed: 21mph (35km/hr)

Crew: 5

Date entered service: 1944

Claim to fame: Most heavily armored German tank of World War II

Above: **The ability of the Tiger II's 180mm thick frontal armor to absorb punishment is graphically illustrated here.**

one way to break out of this vicious circle. These were also known as hollow charge (HC), or *Hohllandung* (HI) by the Germans. As the name implies, this type of round employed a high explosive charge shaped in such a way as to focus the energy of the explosion against the armor plate of a tank and force a narrow jet of hot molten metal through into the interior of the vehicle. Such a hit caused horrendous injuries to the target tank's crew and major damage to the vehicle's interior.

Unlike KE rounds, HEAT was not dependent on velocity to punch through armor, so it could be fired from low velocity weapons, such as short-barrelled howitzers, though the low velocity in turn meant HEAT was not as accurate over long ranges as KE rounds. HEAT technology also spurred the development of low-cost, short-range, hand-held anti-tank weapons, such as the Bazooka, the British PIAT, and German *Panzerfaust* and *Panzerschreck*. These weapons gave infantry a fighting chance against any tanks that came within 100 yards.

The fielding of HEAT rounds inevitably led to the development of counter-measures. Perhaps the most

famous of these were the armor skirts, or *Schürzen*, fitted to the turrets and hulls of German tanks. The idea was that the thin skirt armor would detonate the HEAT round prematurely before it made contact with the tank's main armor, so its deadly design would malfunction. In 1944 British and American tank crews improvised their own answer to HEAT rounds by fitting walls of sandbags around their Shermans.

Whole families of HEAT weapons were developed, including rounds for tanks, artillery pieces, rocket launchers and mines. These last were either buried and detonated under a tank or could be attached magnetically to a tank's hull. The Germans responded to this threat by coating their tanks in anti-magnetic paste, called *Zimmerit*, to make it impossible for any dare-devil Soviet or Allied infantrymen to succeed in their suicide missions.

In tandem with the dramatic advances in armor and gun technology during World War II, tank designers

Right: **German *Volkssturm* home guardsmen arm themselves with *Panzerfaust* rocket launchers. This was the first "throw-away" anti-tank weapon with a HEAT warhead.**

Far right: **Rearming a German Panzer IV. Keeping tanks supplied with fuel and ammunition during tank battles was a constant challenge.**

also sought to mature other areas of their products to improve the fighting edge, ergonomics and ease of manufacture. Bitter experience during the first years of the war taught tank designers that if crews were to survive in battle, serious attention had to be given to the layout of a tank's interior and the jobs each crewman had to perform. It quickly became apparent that one- or two-man turrets were far from satisfactory. If a commander had to load ammunition or aim the tank's armament then he could not be doing his job of navigating the tank or finding targets properly. Likewise, if anything like a decent rate of fire—two or three rounds a minute—was to be achieved then the tank had to have a dedicated loader. The optimum tank crew in most armies became a commander, gunner, loader, driver, and possibly a radio operator/hull machine gunner.

Ergonomics played a vital part in determining the speed at which a target could be engaged. The number of switches and dials the gunner had to use had to be kept to an absolute minimum. In the Sherman, for example, the gunner used his hands to control the switches that elevated the main armament and rotated the turret, while the triggers for the main armament and co-axial machine guns were simple foot pedals. The gunner was kept up to date about whether there was a round loaded in the main armament by means of simple slap on the back from the loader.

A major factor in the development of the tank as a practical weapon system during World War II was the maturity of fire control systems to allow crews to find targets and aim their weapons against them effectively, while remaining protected inside their vehicle. As the war progressed, it became the norm for all crew members of tanks to be provided with optical vision devices or periscopes to give them a view of the outside world. The use of protective metal hoods and hardened glass meant enemy fire could not be directed inside the vehicle, as was the case with World War I tanks. Roof mounted periscopes also meant the integrity of the tank's armor was not weakened by the cutting of holes for vision slits. Tank commanders were provided with 360-degree observation by means of special cupolas, with multiple vision blocks or rotation mechanisms. These allowed the tank commander to hunt for targets and orientate himself properly with friendly tanks.

Tank gunnery was also dependent on the type of observation equipment available and this evolved considerably during the war. A major factor in tank gunnery is correct range estimation. This allows the gunner to adjust his fire to get his shells on target. At the start of the war the most common method of range estimation, for all armies, was fall of shot. As the name suggests, this involved firing a round, watching it impact, and adjusting the aim point to compensate for how far it missed that target by. Not surprisingly this left a lot to be desired. It could be a lengthy exercise, involving the expenditure of valuable or scarce ammunition. Also it alerted the enemy to an opponent's presence and was of limited utility against moving targets.

Various technical methods were introduced to try to overcome the problems of range estimation. Stadiametric was an optical method that involved marking the gunner's sight with the dimensions of various types of targets, such as the enemy's principal tanks and, depending on how they compared with what he could see, the gunner could estimate the range and sight his shot accordingly. The next approach was the use of so-called stereoscopic sights, which used a prism and lens system to provide the gunner with two views of the target. When the gunner adjusted the sight and made the two views merge, he could read a dial that gave him the range to the target. A similar system called coincidence was also developed. These two systems made only a limited appearance on the battlefields of World War II. Prototype stereoscopic systems were used

in late model Panther tanks but few other types benefited from them.

Tank gunners were provided with telescopic sights with a very narrow field of view to allow them to concentrate on particular targets. There were two main types of sights, tube and periscope. Tube sights were mounted along the main gun, so they were almost aligned with it. This reduced the chance of error creeping into the system but increased the vulnerability of the tank because the gun mantle armor had to have a hole in it for the sight. Roof periscopes got round this problem, but were more expensive and complex.

An essential part of a tank's fire control system was an effective crew communication system. All armies eventually provided their tank crews with intercom systems, with throat microphones and head sets. This allowed them to talk above the noise of the vehicle and pass targeting information. All armies, except for the Soviet and Japanese, also provided their tanks with individual radios from the start of the war, so they could work together, locating targets, co-ordinating fire and masking themselves from threats behind terrain.

Firing accurately on the move was beyond the fire control systems of the World War II era, except for the

luckiest of shots. Tanks had to stop to fire accurately. The U.S. Army introduced electrical gun stabilization in elevation onto the Stuart, Lee and Sherman tanks and it was a major advance. It allowed gunners to keep their tank's main armament trained on target as they moved. When the tank stopped, it significantly reduced the time, to a matter of seconds, that the gunner would need to lay the main armament on target and fire.

The speed at which the tank could engage targets was determined largely by the speed at which its turret could be slewed onto the aim point and the main armament elevated or depressed. As tank guns and turrets got heavier then the need for powered traverse became overwhelming. This also raised safety issues because of the fire risks associated with using hydraulic traversing mechanisms.

Ammunition storage and disposal of spent cases needed to be addressed. This also raised safety issues. While storage of ammunition in the turret or the cradle that rotated with the turret greatly eased loading, it also made the rounds harder to protect and prone to explode if the tank's armor was penetrated.

Tank mobility was transformed during World War II by the development of new powerplants, transmissions, suspension systems and track designs. As tanks got bigger and heavier it was necessary to upgrade these elements to ensure they retained their mobility. As with firepower and armor, the T-34 and Panther showed dramatic leaps forward in tank design. Their wide tracks, diesel engines and torsion bar suspension systems allowed them to move across country at very respectable speeds. By using wide tracks they had very small ground pressure ratios, less than a typical man, so they could drive across soft snow or sand and not sink.

The Soviets were keen to give their tanks good river crossing capabilities because of their poor road networks, and designed the T-34 so it could ford through more than 4ft of water. The Germans also wanted to give their heavy Tiger tanks a wading capability because their heavy weight meant few bridges could bear them safely. They fitted the Tiger I with a large snorkel that allowed the tank to wade down to almost 13ft in depth. However, there was an accompanying complex procedure to waterproof the tank, so wading was not really an assault procedure.

The challenge of the D-Day landings led the British to look at transforming their tanks into amphibious assault vehicles. This was achieved by the fitting of a large buoyancy skirt, and a propeller linked to the tank's transmission. This duplex drive resulted in the name DD Sherman. Once ashore the crew could drop the skirt in a matter of seconds and then operate

Right: **The devastated remains of a German Sturmtiger. Only 10 of these monsters, armed with 380mm demolition rocket launchers, were ever built.**

Top right: **Specialist engineer tanks, such as these Churchill Armoured Vehicles Royal Engineers (AVREs), helped ensure British troops suffered minimal casualties during the D-Day landings, unlike the American troops who lacked these vehicles and suffered horrendous losses on Omaha beach.**

Far right: **A DD "swimming" Sherman tank is launched from a landing craft. Bad weather made this vehicle liable to swamping.**

entirely normally. The U.S. Army also used this innovation and, in spite of heavy seas that swamped many DD Shermans, they proved invaluable on D-Day. The U.S. Marine Corps took the amphibious armored vehicle idea one step further and created the LTV, which was propelled through water by its tracks.

As the size and shape of armored divisions evolved during World War II, all armies looked at ways to provide support for their armored spearheads. It was clearly recognized that supporting elements of armored divisions had to be provided with the same degree of mobility and armored protection if the cohesion of the formation and the rate of advance was to be maintained. It was recognized that supporting infantry, artillery, anti-tank, anti-aircraft, engineer, communications, reconnaissance and headquarters units therefore needed their own armored vehicles

The U.S. and German armies at first led the way in this field with their M3 and SdKfz 250/251 series half

tracks. By the middle of the war many of these specialist roles were migrating to fully tracked chassis in many armies. In the German and British armies obsolete tanks were quickly converted to self-propelled artillery and anti-tank roles. In the final year of the war the British went one step further and began converting old Ram tanks, Canadian-made M3/M4 derivatives, into the first fully tracked armored personnel carriers. Nicknamed Kangaroos, these were basically tanks with their turrets removed to allow up to a dozen infantrymen to be carried into battle in relative safety. This created the precedent for the post-World War II generation of armored personnel carriers.

In the early war years the Germans recognized that aircraft might be very effective tank killers if specialist weapons could be developed for them. In the *Blitzkrieg* years, the *Luftwaffe's* Stukas had relied on dive-bombing but it proved not to be accurate enough. They then moved to provide their Ju 87 Stukas, and then Henschel Hs 129s, with long-barrel high velocity cannons. These proved very effective on the Eastern Front in 1943. Stuka ace Ulli Rudel alone claimed 518 tank kills his time on the Eastern Front. The USAAF and the British Royal Air Force on the other hand, turned to rockets as their tank-killing weapon of choice, usually carried in heavy ground-attack fighter aircraft like the P-47 Thunderbolt or Hawker Typhoon. Each 3-inch rocket could be devastating even for the most heavily armored Panther or Tiger. They were fired in volleys to compensate for their accuracy problems. Fewer than one in ten actually found its mark but the paralyzing effect of air attack on German tank movement was considerable.

Experience of Battle

Tank crewmen during World War II had a very different experience than their counterparts during World War I. They fought a rapidly moving war with powerful weapons. Tanks crews clashed with their rivals in deadly duels that resulted in sudden and violent deaths. Tank commanders had to learn how to co-ordinate the actions of large formations, to bring maximum firepower to bear on the enemy and to maintain the momentum of advance.

Above right: **British Bren Gun Carriers move to counter German armor in France during May 1940.**

Left: **Rocket-armed British Typhoon fighter-bombers terrorized German Panzer crews in Normandy during the summer of 1944, making movement in the open by daylight very dangerous.**

Blitzkrieg

During the first two years of the *Blitzkrieg* advances in Europe, German Panzer commanders took apart their opponents in a matter of months. The Germans, however, did not have things all their own way. Oberst Heinrich Eberbach, commander of Panzer Regiment 35, recounted his unit's encounter with French heavy tanks in May 1940 as its pushed westwards from the Meuse:

"During the battle of Merdrop, in the front line the Panzer IIIs and IVs of the 8th Company started a fire fight with readily identified tanks on the eastern edge of Merdrop at a range of about 1,000 meters. Hits were observed from Panzer IVs firing while stationary at stationary targets. The effects could not readily be determined because the regiment didn't move through Merdrop. On the contrary, several 7.5cm armor-piercing shells were clearly seen to bounce off. The enemy tanks presented their front. As the actions progressed, the fire was again taken up at about 600 meters against stationary enemy tanks showing both their fronts and sides. Direct hits were obtained to good effect. Three enemy tanks lay knocked out, one catching fire.

"After this, two enemy tanks driving from left to right were fired on at a range of 900 meters. At first it was observed that we fired too short and with too little lead (speed of enemy tanks about 15 to 20 km/hr). With 15 to 20 rounds, both were knocked out after driving about 100 meters.

"After the regiment moved past the north edge of Merdrop 11 enemy tanks came out of Merdrop and attacked the following motorized infantry. The 1st Battalion immediately turned around and fired at the enemy tanks at a range of 400 to 600 meters. Eight tanks remained stationary: three escaped. An enemy tank climbing a rise was shot by 2cm, 3.7cm and 7.5cm tank guns at a range of about 800 meters. A large number of hits including 7.5cm, were readily observed. The tank wasn't stopped by these hits and disappeared behind the rise. Later it was found undamaged, struck in a defile. Gouges left by a large number of hits were evident. It was a Somua with very strong armor, a 4.7cm gun and one machine gun.

"When it reached the height between Jandrain and Jandrenouille, the regiment came under fire from enemy tanks on the next height to the west, from anti-tank guns in Jandrenouille, and from machine guns in Jandrain. The regiment couldn't advance further due to ammunition shortages because it had fired too often at ranges over 800 yards. The 3rd Company and scouting platoon sent to clean out Jandrain, knocked out five

Hotchkiss tanks at close range with 2cm guns, took over 400 prisoners and captured four anti-tank guns and numerous machine guns." [1]

As German Panzer spearheads raced across France they threatened to cut the British off from the mass of the French Army covering Paris. On May 21, 1940, the British 50th Division, under the command of tank pioneer, Major-General Giffard le Q. Martel, was ordered to counterattack to try open a corridor to the south. He had the 4th and 7th Battalions of the Royal Tank Regiment, with 58 Mark I and 16 Mark II Matilda Infantry tanks, supported by some 70 French Somua S-35 medium tanks, to take on Erwin Rommel's 7th Panzer Division with 180 tanks. The regimental history of the Durham Light Infantry (DLI) takes up the story of the first large-scale tank battle of World War II:

"The [DLI] Battalions had to start moving almost as soon as they received their orders and arrangements for co-operation with the tanks—of which no one had had any previous experience—had also to be made as they moved forward. Moreover, very little was known about the exact position of the Germans and there was no further time for reconnaissance.

"Both the 6th and 8th [DLI] Battalions started off at 11.30am but neither reached the Arras–Doullens road at the appointed time for the very simple reason that the Germans were in fact in positions to the north of it. The 4th Royal Tank Regiment, who preceded the 6th Battalion, met the enemy almost at once to the west of Dainville. They shot up his transport and killed many men, and the 6th Battalion was able to clear up the area round Dainville and take several hundred dejected prisoners. This initial success put new heart into everyone and offset the fatigue of the last days' marching. But it caused a delay and the Battalion did not reach its start line till 3.30pm—an hour and half later. By 5 pm it had occupied Beaurains.

"The 8th Battalion was less fortunate, and in fact never reached the start line at all. The 7th Royal Tank Regiment, supporting it, moved off too soon and disappeared in the distance. That was the last the Battalion saw of it. But when the leading troops reached the Arras–St Pol road they saw striking evidence that the tanks had passed that way. German vehicles, burnt out and damaged, were strewn all over the road. Enemy dead lay where they had fallen." [2]

Right: The German 25th Panzer Regiment at the height of the *Blitzkrieg* across France, with Panzer IV leading the way for a posse of PzKpfw 38(t). This was the German version of the Czech TNH P-S light tank.

Eventually Rommel was able to cobble together a defense, mustering a gun line of 105mm howitzers and 88mm Flak guns to fight off 7th Royal Tank Regiment. "With the enemy tanks so dangerously close only rapid fire from every gun could save the situation" recalled Rommel. "We ran from gun to gun. I brushed aside the commander's objections that the range was too great." By nightfall Rommel's 25th Panzer Regiment was able to counterattack and the British armor fell back, leaving 46 ruined tanks behind.

Operation Barbarossa

On June 22, 1941, Hitler unleashed his Panzer force eastwards against Stalin's Russia. The disorganized and badly led Red Army was soon in full scale retreat, leaving the majority of their 17,000 tanks behind. While the German advance soon trapped millions of Soviet soldiers in huge pockets, small groups of Red Army tanks fought tenaciously when cornered. German units could suddenly find themselves fighting for their lives as heavily armored T-34 and KV-1 tanks rampaged among them. Panzer Regiment 6 found itself under heavy attack in this way in the fighting near Smolensk:

"On 19th August, towards 0530 hours, strong Russian forces attacked the city of Unjetscha from the northwest and attempted to cross the bridge and push into the city with six T-34 heavy tanks. Several Panzers of the 1st and 2nd Battalions were in the city awaiting repair. Lieutenant Bueschen drove with two Panzer IIIs to the northwest exit of the city to repulse the enemy tank attack in front of the bridge. A Panzer IV was already in firing position there and had immobilized a heavy Russian tank by a hit in the road wheel. The crew jumped out and fled. The Panzer IV was hit by another attacking Russian tank. Two of them were immobilized about 70 meters in front of the bridge by a Panzer III. Their crews also abandoned the tanks. In spite of heavy fire, a further tank managed to get over the bridge and into the city. A Panzer III drove after him with Lieutenant Stoerk on board. They caught up with the tank at the railway embankment, immobilized the tank, and set it on fire by throwing balled explosives into the motor compartment. The crew, including a first lieutenant, were captured. When captured the first lieutenant said that the attack had been conducted with 15 tanks."[3]

By the winter of 1942 the Germans were on the defensive, after a major Soviet offensive had surrounded the Sixth Army at Stalingrad. Oberst Helmut Ritgen's 11th Panzer Regiment, was ordered to spearhead the relief effort, Operation Winter Tempest, to punch a corridor through to the 290,000 trapped German troops. He describes the early stages of the attack:

"Attacking with the westering sun to their backs the tanks rolled at top speed towards the enemy, their tracks throwing up glittering clouds of snow in the low flat light. After crossing a road we came to a hill. There was the enemy. 'Sand fountains' were splashing up, devilish close—one impact after another. The difficult ground delayed our charge: our guns replied to the Soviet fire, but the range was extreme and the targets tiny and hard to make out. The defense included 76.2mm anti-tank guns and anti-tank rifles. Several of our tanks were hit. Although some of the enemy guns were silenced, a further charge would cost unnecessary high casualties: the commanding officer therefore ordered all tanks back to hull-down

positions, where they turned to the right in order to force the anti-tank front further south.

"Again the tanks charged towards the enemy positions, but the leading vehicles hesitated. It was essential that the attack kept up its momentum; we had to achieve a breakthrough, and not wait for support to arrive. Lieutenant Michael took the lead, dragging other tanks after him by force of example, and rolled on at top speed ignoring fire which was concentrated on the leading vehicles. A few minutes seemed to last an eternity—but suddenly we were in among the excellently concealed enemy positions, with Soviets fighting desperately all around us. There were anti-tank guns to the right, to the left, and straight ahead. We rolled over them. The attack was irresistible. Panic-stricken Soviets attempted to retreat in all directions. We left the mopping up to the Panzergrenadiers and went storming on to the east."[4]

Below left and Below: **StuG III assault guns were increasingly pressed into action to replace tanks with the German armored forces because they could be produced quicker and more cheaply than turreted armored fighting vehicles.**

Right and Far right: **Russian T-34s prepare for a winter assault against the Germans on the Eastern Front.**

North Africa

In 1941 Hitler ordered two divisions, later designated as 15th and 21st Panzer Divisions, to North Africa to turn back the British Eighth Army, which had almost pushed the Italian forces out of Libya. For the next two years British and German tank units fought a fast moving battle in the North African desert that was to enter the legends of armored warfare. The open terrain made this a war of maneuver, with tank units sweeping across the desert looking for open flanks. Tank commanders had to think quickly to take advantage of fleeting opportunities. The sudden appearance of enemy tanks on a flank could spell disaster, because it meant weak side armor was vulnerable, while a commander who engaged his opponents from a hull-down firing position, with only his turrets showing, made it far more difficult for the enemy to return fire effectively.

Lieutenant Joachim Schorm, a Panzer III commander with Panzer Regiment 5, spearheaded a German attack on the British garrison of Tobruk on April 14, 1941:

"600 meters off on the reverse slope, anti-tank guns. 900 meters distant, in the hollow behind is a tank. Behind that next dip, 1,200 meters away another tank. How many? I see only the effect of the fire on the terraced-like dispositions of the enemy. Judging from their width and thickness these must be at least 12 guns. Above us Italian

fighter planes come into the fray. Two of them crash in our midst. The optical instruments are spoilt with dust. Nevertheless I register several unmistakable hits. A few anti-tank guns are silenced, some enemy tanks are burning. Just then we are hit, and the wireless smashed to bits. Now our communications are cut off. What is more our ammunition is running out. I follow the battalion commanders. Our attack is fading out. From every side the superior forces of the enemy shoot at us.

"'Retire.' There is a crash, just behind us. The engine and gasoline tank are in the rear. The tank must be on fire. I turn around and look through the slit. It is not burning. Our luck is holding. Poor 8th Machine Gunners! We take a wounded man and two others abroad, and the other tanks do the same. Most of the men have bullet wounds. With its last strength my tank follows the others which we lose from time to time in the dust clouds. But we have to press on towards the south, as it is the only way through. Good God! Supposing we don't find the way? And the engines won't do any more!

"Close on our right and left flanks the English tanks shoot into our midst. We are struck in the tracks of the tank, which creak and groan. The lane is in sight. Everything hastens towards it. English anti-tank guns shoot into the mass. Our own anti-tank positions and the 8.8cm anti-aircraft guns are almost deserted, but the crews are lying silently beside them. Italian artillery which was to have protected our left flank lies, equally

deserted. English troops run out of their positions, some shooting at us with machine pistols, some with hands raised. With drawn pistols they are compelled to enter our tanks. The English machine guns start up and the prisoners fling themselves to the ground. 1st Lieutenant v. Huelsen and my machine gunner lie on that side of my tank which faces towards the machine gun battalion. We go on, now comes the gap—now the ditch! The driver cannot see a thing for dust, nor I either. We drive by instinct. The tank almost gets stuck in the two ditches, blocking the road: but manages to extricate itself with great difficulty. With their last reserves of power, the crew gets out of range and returns to camp. Examine damage to tank. My men remove an armor-piercing high explosive shell from the right-hand auxiliary gasoline tank; 3cm of armor plate bogie cut clear through. The fuel tank shot away. The fuel had run out to this level without igniting! Had it not been for the bogie we should not have got out alive."[5]

Major Hohmann, commanding 2nd Battalion, 5th Panzer Regiment, led 27 tanks into action during Operation Brevity on the Libyan border on May 15, 1941:

"The Panzer Battalion was alerted at 0600 hours. At 0710, the Battalion met up with a reconnaissance element several kilometers south of Point 206, then turned east and attacked a group of enemy tanks advancing towards Capuzzo [A Squadron and Headquarters 4th Royal Tank Regiment, with eleven (Matilda) Mk II and four Mk VI light tanks]. I sent the message: 'British Mark II tanks are attacking. Request 8.8cm Flak to Capuzzo.' The engagement with about 16 Mark II infantry tanks was obstinately fought. In this action two Mark II infantry tanks were observed to be immobilized. We didn't manage to stop the enemy or to force him to turn away from his objective because of the negligible effect of our weapons. I couldn't implement the tactics that had the best chance of success against the Mark II tanks, concentrated fire at close range from several 5cm tank guns, because of the small number of Panzers available. I only saw the risk of being forced to the west and cut off from the main

battlefield. By radio message I then ordered: 'Turn left, follow commander Meissel.' The heavy tank combat made it difficult to break contact. Because of their high speed Staff of 5 Company and three Panzers of 6 Company reached the border fence south of Capuzzo. The order was not received [by all our tanks] due to failure of a radio set, resulting in 14 Panzers of the 6th and 8th Company turning west, Having lost radio contact with the Battalion they later moved back to Sidi Azeiz, under the command of Captain Müller.

"At 0825 hours in the area of the border fence south of Capuzzo a firefight again occurred between Mark II infantry tanks and 12 Panzers remaining with the battalion. The Mark II tanks pulled back. The battalion slowly moved back towards Capuzzo and encountered truck-borne British infantry, who were forced to take cover by machine gun fire."[6]

British tank units fought back ferociously, even though they often had inferior equipment. A Squadron, 9th Lancers, turned and snapped against its pursuers in this way during the preparations for the Battle of El Alamein in October 1942.

"On the 16th, A Squadron, on the left, rang up to say that there were some suspicious-looking vehicles in front, and could these be attacked? The Colonel gave permission and the remainder of the regiment then witnessed as nice a bit of tank handling as ever seen. Twelve graceful, putty-coloured cruisers were standing in a semi-circle, their guns pointing inquiringly towards the west where a column of dust rose on the still air. Behind stood in line the close support tanks of squadron headquarters. Suddenly all four fired, their guns elevated high and shells making an arc of smoke trail in the sky, and there was a puff of blue smoke behind each tank as their engines started. The 3-inch guns were firing smoke as hard as they could be loaded and after the fourth salvo the line began to move, slowly at first until, gathering speed, each tank was throwing up a plume of sand. The squadron disappeared in a cloud of dust. The watchers saw no more, but from the bank of dust could be heard the slam of tank guns and rapid hammer of Besas. For ten minutes the curtain remained drawn and then A squadron came slowly back through the clearing smoke. The Colonel's cruiser nosed its way to them and stopped as each tank swung around to face west again."[7]

Right: **German armor gathers prior to the Battle of Kursk in July 1943. This proved to be the biggest tank battle of the war, when almost 6,000 German and Russian tanks and heavy assault guns met in battle.**

Far East

The Japanese were keen exponents of using their small number of tanks to support infantry attacks. Colonel Masanobu Tsuji was in the advance wave of the Saeki Detachment during its attack on the Changlun River in Malaya on December 10, 1941:

"Enemy shells luckily deadened the noise of our tanks, and the torrential rain concealed us. Ten medium tanks cut ahead of the Saeki Detachment, crossing the bridge which had been repaired, evaded shells while enemy machine-gun bullets rebounded from their armor, and advanced like angry cattle running amok. Lieutenant Colonel Saeki in a black motor car captured from the enemy immediately followed after the medium tanks. Bullets came flying from left and right. After travelling about two kilometers we came upon a mystery. Ten guns with their muzzles turned towards us were lined up on the road, but beside them we could not find even one man of their crews. The enemy appeared to be sheltering from the heavy rain under the rubber trees, but fire issuing from sentries' huts or from tents gave the impression of coming from a formidable adversary. Our tanks were already on the road and twenty or so enemy armored cars ahead were literally trampled underfoot. It was a hand-to-hand fight which seemed to overstep the bounds of common sense. On each side of the road there was a deep drainage ditch and a high embankment. The enemy armored cars could not escape by running away, and were sandwiched between our medium tanks. The distance to the enemy was so close that cannon and machine gun could not be brought to bear against one another. It was speed and weight of armor that decided the issue.

"Without casting a glance at the remnants of the enemy among the rubber trees on both sides of the road, for the second time the medium tanks were rushed to head of the column. Everything was now pitch black. With the lamps of the tanks shining immediately in front on the track of advance, we came across several bridges. At each of them we alighted from the car. Without exception preparations were made for their demolition—the explosive charges were laid and the electric wires connected. Promptly cutting these wires with our sabres, we hurried on the advance, thus nipping in the bud the destruction of about ten bridges."[8]

Merril B. Twining, Operations Officer of 1st Marine Division on the island of Guadalcanal, however, recalled that Japanese tanks were not invincible. On October 21, 1942, his 3rd Battalion, 1st Marine Regiment, turned back a major Japanese tank attack:

"The Marines had spent the day improving their positions and held fast. 'After all,' as one youngster modestly explained to me, 'where the hell could you go?' When the artillery fire lifted, a company of Japanese attacks supported by infantry attempted to storm the sand-spit as a prelude to their well known 'filtering attack.' They intended to send the tanks straight down the 'government track' to disrupt our only line of communications while their massed infantry followed in great depth on a narrow front. This had to be stopped at the outset. It was. Anti-tank fire from our half-tracks swept the bar. Careful pre-ranged and precisely registered artillery concentrations commenced on signal. One tank made it across the sand-spit and crashed through our wire. Private First Class Joseph D.R. Champagne reached out of his foxhole and placed a hand grenade on the tread of the tank stopped beside him. The explosion partially disabled the tank. It was destroyed by 75mm fire from a nearby half track. The sand-spit was littered with the wreckage of nine hostile tanks and numerous enemy dead."[9]

Kursk

In July 1943 the might of the Red Army and Wehrmacht clashed at Kursk, as Hitler tried to regain the initiative after the defeat of his Sixth Army at Stalingrad. More than 2,500 German tanks and assault guns went into battle against some 3,300 Soviet tanks and fought for more than ten days until Hitler called a halt to Operation Citadel. His *Blitzkrieg* had failed to break the Red Army, leaving it free to resume the offensive.

General Pavel Rotmistrov, commander of 5th Guards Tank Army, led his 800 tanks into battle on July 12 to halt the advance of the élite II SS Panzer Corps:

"I raised my binoculars and saw our famous T-34s leaving cover and rushing ahead, gathering speed. At the same time, I caught sight of a host of enemy tanks. Apparently, both we and Germans had launched our offensives simultaneously. I was surprised to see how close to each other both Germans and our tanks had been moving. The two tank armadas were set for a head-on collision. The rising sun blinded the German tank crews but clearly outlined the Nazi tanks for our guns.

Right and Over page: **Heavily armored Tiger Is first saw action in late 1942 and instantly gained a reputation among Allied tank crews as formidable opponents.**

"In a few minutes the first echelon tanks of our 29th and 18th Corps were firing on the move, clashing into and breaking the formations of the German troops, The Germans seemed to be surprised to encounter such a large number of our tanks and to be attacked so resolutely. Control of the forward enemy tanks had been disrupted and the enemy Tigers and Panthers, denied fire superiority in close combat, were attacked at close range by Soviet T-34 and even T-70 tanks. The battlefield was enveloped in smoke and dust and the earth shaken by strong blasts. Tanks clashed, and locked together could no longer discharge. They fought until one caught fire or came to a halt with a torn track. But even disabled tanks kept firing as long as they could.

"The tanks seemed to be caught in a giant whirlpool. Our T-34s, maneuvering and running circles around the enemy, shot Tigers and Panthers at close range but then they themselves, caught in the direct line of fire of heavy enemy tanks and self-propelled guns, would catch fire and perish. Shells striking strong armor whined off, tracks were torn to pieces, rollers were shot away by direct hits, and ammunition was detonating inside tanks, blowing off their turrets.

"A large group of German Tiger tanks attacked the 2nd Battalion of the 181st Brigade of the 18th Tank Corps. The battalion commander, Captain Skripkin, boldly joined the battle. He personally hit two enemy tanks and having caught the third machine in his sights, pulled the trigger, but at that moment his tank

was hit and caught fire. As the driver, Master Sergeant Nikilayev, and the wireless operator Zyryanov pulled the gravely wounded battalion commander out of the tank, they saw a Tiger rolling towards them. Zyryanov dragged the Captain to cover in a shell crater, while Nikilayev and loader Chernov jumped back into the burning tank and slammed it into the enemy tank, They perished, having fulfilled their duty to the end." [10]

On the other side of the Prokhorovka battlefield, Hubert Neuzert, was commanding a Marder III anti-tank gun or *Panzerjäger* of the Waffen-SS *Leibstandarte Adolf Hitler* Panzergrenadier Division;

"Then suddenly there were 40 or 50 T-34s coming at us from the right. We had to turn and open fire on them.

All of a sudden three bold giants among them raced off across the basin towards the collective farm They captured the road leading to it. I did not have a chance to fire. So we had to shift positions through the farm buildings. I had barely taken aim when I had to fire at my first T-34. My shell went past it and the shell case got stuck in the gun. I ducked between the houses once again and I was in front of one when I got the mechanism unjammed. A T-34 appeared right in front of me when my assistant gunner yelled so loud that I could hear him without headphones, 'Shell in the barrel.' That on top of everything else! I swivelled around to face the T-34 racing towards us at a distance of about 150 meters, when the next tragedy struck. The rear support for the gun collapsed, and the barrel swung up to the sky. I used the force of swivelling the turret to *bring the barrel of my 7.5cm gun down, managed to get the T-34 turret in my sights and fired. A hit! The hatch opened and two men jumped out. One stayed put, while the other hopped across the road between the houses about thirty meters in front of me. I hit the T-34 again. Everywhere, there were shells of burning tanks. Standing in a sector about 1,500 meters wide about ten or twelve artillery pieces were smoldering. One hundred twenty tanks were supposed to have been in the attack; there could well have been more."* [11]

Hauptsturmführer Tieman, who was in command of the 7th Company of the *Leibstandarte's* Panzer regiment during this battle, recalled:

"Then began a period of very hard combat, consisting of an all-round mad defense striking out to all sides, often without resupply for an entire day. The Russians were trying to cut off our Panzer wedge from the east and north with masses of their tanks. There were tanks day and night. Four battles in one day. Then we were pulled back. With only half my Panzers, and some of them in tow, I returned to point of departure for this attack in the dark pouring rain. I had never experienced war like that, in combat against enemy tanks outnumbering us by a factor of ten. It was a furious battle of biting in and chewing fast. Our regiment destroyed 62 enemy tanks on this one day. My company, which made the first contact with the enemy, destroyed twenty itself. Until today they had only destroyed 43 in total. But I lost only one Panzer in the company. The company has become a pledged brotherhood. There is an esprit de corps and a good spirit here: it could pull up trees by the roots. My Panzer was hit once. I got out of it in time, but the radio operator was wounded. Now my Panzer, my trusty 705 is back in the repair shop." [12]

Northwest Europe

The invasion of Normandy in June 1944 saw U.S. and British tank crews pitted against veteran German Panzer units. Allied tankmen, such as John Foley, a Churchill tank troop commander, found themselves locked in a deadly duel with far superior opponents:

"Being in reserve we didn't see anything … but we could hear Mike Carter's troops blazing away over the crest of the hill and we could hear his somewhat puzzled voice reporting over the air [radio] that these enormous great Tiger tanks managed to hide themselves remarkably well. That was the point at which Mike's tank seemed to sit back suddenly on its rear bogies,

tongues of flame shot out of the engine compartment. Four figures leaped out of the tank into the clouds of black, oily smoke which were now pouring from the burning vehicle. In Five Troop, hatches were gingerly opened and we stared in breathless awe at the burning tank. This was the first time we had seen the phenomenon casually referred to as 'brewing up,' although we were due to see a lot more. The blazing hulk vibrated with the crash of ammunition exploding in the bins, and feathery plumes of white smoke arched out of the open hatchways as the smoke bombs caught fire." [13]

German historian Paul Carrell's description of the Battle of Tilly, on June 11, makes it clear that the Normandy battlefront was not a forgiving place:

"The armored reserves of the Panzer Lehr Division now mounted their counterattack. The steel colossi of Panthers and Tigers rattled through the narrow streets. Second Lieutenant Theo was a troop commander in the 6th Company and the Skipper of the third tank that bore the code name Lemon. Attentively he watched his front. Ahead of him, advancing in single file along the narrow farm track, were three tanks of the company. Now they turned left. They skirted the edge of the wood, rumbled past the tangle of tall hedgerows, clumps of shrubs, thick patches of undergrowth, and gnarled old apple trees. Now the three tanks in front were bumping across an open field into the wood. Instantly all hell broke loose.

"'Enemy armor! Turret 11 o'clock! Fire!' These were the commands Second Lieutenant Theo heard in his earphones. They were the orders of the skippers of the tanks ahead of him. A loud bang. Theo entered the open field. And now he could see what had happened. On the path leading into the wood stood a smoking Cromwell tank shot up by Cherry. Billows of smoke rising behind the wreck suggested that other Cromwells, those new, highly mobile British tanks, were withdrawing under cover of a smoke-screen. Suddenly a Sherman burst from the hedge on the right, but immediately turned tail and vanished in the thick undergrowth. Theo sent a shell behind him. Almost at once he found himself under fire from the left. He turned his gun towards the outline of a tank just behind a hedge. Direct hit. There was no movement from the direction of his victim. Evidently the crew had already abandoned the tank." [14]

Ken Trout, a Sherman gunner with the 1st Northamptonshire Yeomanry, recalled what it was like to stalk a German tank through the hedgerows:

"The SLAM-CRASH of an aimed shot—direct, violent, massive—smashes across the humdrum background of barrage. Where? What? '2 Baker. I am bloody hit!' 'Bail out!' 'Hornet at … Gawd' God that's Astley gone! 'Hornet—enemy tank or SP? Where? Where? Where, where, where … I squeeze the grip right … left … traversing quickly, staring into the camel shaped trees. 'Hornet at … where, where … 'The hedge, solid-topped, fairly level … has a gap, a gap. A gap. Why? What? 'Charlie, left of roof Hornet in hedge over … ' I adjust left, down, crosswires on! Stamp [the Sherman's gun trigger was a foot pedal]. Flame at muzzle. Frustrating smoke. Smoke! Smoke! Clearing to show spark of tracer leaping high into the gap but another tracer from near gully flies into gap ahead of my tracer as Stan slaps my leg, loaded, down a bit, fire! Stan slaps. Stamp. Fire. Traverse. Sight. Slap. Stamp. Fire. Other flashes than mine festoon the far hedge with artificial flowers, blooming, dying, red as Flanders poppies. As a feather of smoke, more permanent than transient clouds exhaled by shell bursts, wavers up to the left of the roof. I put my foot on the other pedal as solidly as the accelerators of a car. The co-axial Browning rattles away, every fifth bullet trailing tiny tracer sparks. Other tanks are brassing up the hedge in a similar fashion. Bookie calls 'Look over to the right of the track. More smoke.' There is indeed more smoke, over 2 Troop's position. But it is not the column of flame or pall of hideous, thick, black smoke which marks the total conflagration of a Sherman. This is a thinner, less dense spiral." [15]

Captain James Burt, commanding Company B, 66th Armored Regiment, 2nd Armored Division, won the Medal of Honor for leading a combined armor-infantry attack during the Battle for Aachen in the fall of 1944 as Allied forces approached the borders of Germany. His bravery citation describes graphically that successful tank commanders often had to leave the relative safety of their vehicles to take the war to the enemy:

"In the first day of action, when infantrymen ran into murderous small arms and mortar fire, Captain Burt dismounted from his tank about 200 yards to the rear and moved forward on foot beyond the infantry's position, where, as the enemy concentrated a tremendous volume of fire upon him, he calmly motioned his tanks into good firing positions. As our attack gained momentum, he climbed abroad his tank and directed the action from the rear deck, exposed to hostile volleys which finally wounded him painfully in the face and

neck. He maintained his dangerous post despite point blank self-propelled gunfire until friendly artillery knocked out these enemy weapons, and then proceeded to advance to the infantry scouts' positions to deploy his tanks for the defense of the gains which had been made.

"To direct artillery fire, on 15th October, he took his tank 300 yards into the enemy lines, where he dismounted and remained for one hour giving accurate data to friendly gunners. Twice the tank he was riding was knocked out by enemy action and each time he climbed aboard another vehicle and continued the fight." [16]

The poor armor and firepower of American tanks is clearly demonstrated by historian S.L.A. Marshall's account of the defense of Noville during the Battle of the Bulge, in December 1944. The tank and tank destroyer crews of Major William R. Desobry's task force, of the 20th Armored Infantry Battalion, had to wait until German tanks were at almost suicidal range before taking on the enemy Panthers:

"Quite suddenly the fog lifted like a curtain going up and revealing the stage. The countryside was filled with tanks. From the second story of his command post in the Noville schoolhouse, Captain Omar R. Billet saw at a glance more than 30 tanks. Others saw many more from different points of vantage. In an extended skirmish line along the ridge short of Vaux were 14 tanks. Desobry's men looked at the scene and knew they were facing an entire Panzer division. The leading enemy formations were 1,000 yards away. When they closed to 800 yards out, the 14 tanks on the hill halted and shelled the town. Other tanks were swinging around the right flank but on the left the enemy armor was already within 200 yards of the American positions when the curtain went up.

"Little knots of men on foot were coming up behind the German tanks and the batteries of the U.S. 420th Armored Field Artillery Battalion hammered at those. It is doubtful if the American artillery stopped a single tank. About the time the enemy armor became fully revealed, a platoon from the 609th Tank Destroyer Battalion rolled into Noville, and added the gunpower of its four tank destroyers to guns already shooting. The sudden sharp focus given to the line of Panzer IVs and Vs [Panthers] as the fog cleared along the ridge line made then stand out like ducks in a shooting gallery. Nine were hit straight away, three exploding in flames. One came charging down the highway and was turned into a flaming wreck 500 yards out. At the range of 600 yards an American cavalryman engaged a Panther

with his armored car and knocked it out with one shot from his 37mm gun—the most miraculous hit of the morning. Two tanks which had been close in the foreground, ahead of the ridge, charged the town at a speed that brought momentary confusion to Desobry's command post. But at 30 yards range a 105mm assault gun fired its first round, stopping one tank but not disabling its gun. The German tank fired but missed, then tried to withdraw, but with a quick round the assault gun finished him off. The other German tanks had been stopped by one of Desobry's mediums at a range of 75 yards. Looking in the direction from which they had come, observers in the taller buildings of Noville could see four tanks lying in a draw—almost

concealed. The ground cover was almost enough so the Noville guns couldn't get at them—until one of these tanks made the mistake of pulling out onto the road. It was a shining mark, 300 yards away. A tank destroyer fired and the tank exploded in a blaze. The fog swirled back, screening the draw, and the other three tanks ran off into it."[17]

Below: **A Sherman speeds past a knocked out Panther during the latter stages of the Battle of the Bulge. The Ardennes campaign highlighted the importance of airpower–while the weather was bad and Allied aircraft were unable to fly, the German surprise offensive made good progress. As the weather cleared, Allied fighter-bombers got airborne, and dominated the skies above the attack, destroying German armor and infantry almost with impunity.**

CHAPTER FOUR

THE COLD WAR 1945–89

The Battlefield

For more than four decades much of the world was nominally at peace, as the capitalist west and Communist east were locked in a deadly nuclear stand-off. Known as the Cold War, this period also saw the outbreak of vicious regional conflicts around the globe as so-called super-power proxies vied for local supremacy. In this environment military budgets and technological developments reigned unchecked to fuel the huge nuclear and conventional forces necessary to maintain the "balance of terror."

The ideological confrontation between the United States and its allies on the one hand and the Communist powers led by Moscow and Peking on the other, burst into life in the late 1940s. Soviet dictator Josef Stalin's efforts to control Eastern Europe in the years after the end of World War II and the success of the Chinese Communist Revolution triggered a massive response by the West. When North Korean Communist troops invaded South Korea in 1950 and Chinese troops joined the conflict a few months later, the Cold War suddenly became "hot."

In response to these moves, the United States under President Dwight D. Eisenhower looked to its near monopoly in nuclear weapons as a means to "contain communism." It promulgated the strategy of massive nuclear response as a means of deterring any Communist attack against the U.S. or allied countries. The U.S. developed a wide range of nuclear weapons from massive thermonuclear bombs to destroy cities to small tactical or battlefield nuclear weapons for use against armies, naval task forces or flying bomber formations. Likewise the Soviet Union developed its own arsenal of nuclear war-fighting weapons.

During the early 1960s under the administration of President John F. Kennedy, the U.S. began to move away from "massive retaliation" towards a policy of so-called "flexible response." This was aimed at containing Communism by any means short of nuclear Armageddon. A threat to the U.S. or its allies was now to be countered with a proportionate response and escalation to the use of nuclear weapons would only take place if the Soviets used them, or Allied forces were in danger of total defeat. This began a major rebuilding of NATO forces in Europe from being mere "trip wires" to trigger a nuclear response, into war-fighting forces that would be able to take on and defeat any Soviet attack. By building up a realistic defense capability, it was hoped that the Soviets would be deterred from trying to seize western Europe. Flexible response was built on the premise that the Soviets would not be deterred from attacking a small NATO ally by a U.S. promise of nuclear retaliation. Why would the Americans risk the incineration of Chicago for the sake of Denmark? Or so went the argument.

Outside Europe the confrontation between East and West was played out in a series of regional conflicts or "brushfire wars," which ranged in scope from small scale insurgencies to full blown conflicts. Under Kennedy and later President Lyndon Johnson, the U.S. became drawn into many of these to counter what it perceived as Communist aggression. In some cases the U.S. supplied hardware and "advisors" and in others, such as in Southeast Asia, it became sucked in as a full scale combatant. At the height of the Vietnam war some 500,000 U.S. troops were engaged in the war, fighting on land, in the air and on the sea.

From the mid-1950s to the 1980s there was a spate of what became known as "regional conflicts." These were fuelled by a mix of Cold War political rivalries and deep-seated local religious and ethnic hatred. The Arab-Israeli Wars of 1956, 1967 and 1973 as well as the 1965 and 1971 India-Pakistan wars epitomized this type of conflict. To outside observers they seemed limited in nature, but to the participants they were all-out wars of survival.

Right: **Opposing Force (OPFOR) vehicles at the U.S. Army's National Training Center (NTC) were specially modified to mimic Soviet-designed vehicles, to practise Abrams crews in fighting the latest threats. (STRICOM)**

The American defeat in Vietnam heralded a new phase in the Cold War in the 1970s. Increased Soviet confidence led to expeditions to support revolutionary movements in Ethiopia and Angola. Then in 1979 Soviet troops invaded Afghanistan to crush a revolt by Islamic guerrillas against the pro-Moscow regime in Kabul. For almost a decade some 85,000 Soviet troops were locked into a bloody counter-insurgency campaign. At the same time Soviet forces in the European theater were progressively reinforced with new tanks, armored vehicles, artillery weapons, helicopters, aircraft and tactical nuclear missiles. By the early 1980s the Soviets and their Warsaw Pact allies fielded 20,000 tanks in Europe.

In Washington, under President Ronald Reagan, these events were seen as a major challenge and a counter-buildup was ordered. New weapons began to roll off production lines in large numbers. Huge field exercises were held on either side of the Iron Curtain by NATO and Warsaw Pact forces, involving hundreds of thousands of men. These tested war plans for mobilization and reinforcement, as well as new tactics and operational concepts. Although both sides were careful not to identify an enemy specifically it was very obvious that these were rehearsals for World War III.

At the end of the decade the Soviet Union under Mikhail Gorbachev effectively opted out of the arms race with the U.S.. In November 1989 the people of Berlin pulled down the wall that divided their city. Soviet troops in East Germany, on Moscow's orders, stood by and watched. The Cold War was over.

Even as the Cold War was coming to an end in Europe, the Mid-East remained highly unstable. Iran and Iraq fought a massive conventional war for most of the 1980s. Israeli and Syrian armor clashed in Lebanon in 1982. For the next 18 years Israeli troops were sucked into a low-level conflict with Islamic guerrillas in Lebanon. With wars and conflict proliferating, Mid-Eastern countries became large purchasers of military hardware from both East and West.

Tactical and Doctrinal Development

Not surprisingly, as the world's leading military powers became preoccupied with developing their nuclear arsenals in the decade after the war, the tank was relegated to near the bottom of the pile for resources. From 1945 to the start of the Korean War, armored forces in the U.S., Britain and France developed little and Germany was not permitted to rearm. The appearance of the Soviet Josef Stalin heavy tank in Berlin in 1945 prompted a reaction and ensured continued development of tanks already being produced, such as the M26 Pershing and British Centurion but, as far as tactics and doctrine went, original thinking was not in evidence. The Korean War was largely fought with equipment, doctrine and tactics left over from World War II.

Right: **Israeli Shermans and M3 half tracks form up for the attack on Rafa during the 1967 Six Day War. (IDF Spokesman)**

This state of affairs changed dramatically after the Korean War, although in a direction that perhaps drew more on science fiction rather than practical military reality. In the 1950s U.S. military everything had to have a nuclear angle. The U.S. Army, fearing itself redundant in the age of nuclear bombers and missile firing submarines, decided to reorganize itself around tactical nuclear missiles and artillery. Divisions were reorganized around their nuclear firepower, with infantry and tanks reduced to the status of close protection forces rather than offensive elements in their own right. It was also decided to make these so-called "Pentomic" divisions as small as possible to present as small a target as possible on the nuclear battlefield.

In Britain and Russia similar ideas dominated military thinking during the 1950s and further downgraded the importance of the tank. In his 1957 UK Defence White Paper, Minister for Defence Duncan Sandys planned to slash the size of Britain's conventional forces and forecast the rise of missile warfare. In the Soviet Union, the country's new leader Nikita Khrushchev envisaged conventional ground forces as being useful only for mopping up after nuclear strikes had devastated the enemy.

The Red Army, however, was far more effective at adapting armored warfare to the requirements of the nuclear age than its U.S. or European counterparts. Thanks to the role played by Soviet generals, such as Georgi Zhukov, in supporting Khrushchev after Stalin's death, they were able to secure a large share of defense resources for the modernization of the Red Army's armored forces. Their wartime experience of offensive

saw a revolution in Soviet armored warfare doctrine. Soviet armored forces were seen as strategic weapons to be used to achieve decisive victory at the operational level. They were designed to conduct high-tempo operations over long distances, after first blasting through enemy defenses. Soviet tank divisions were equipped with lavish amounts of self-propelled artillery to help them achieve a breakthrough. BMP infantry fighting vehicles were designed to allow the infantry to keep up with the tank spearheads as they pushed deep behind enemy lines. Mil Mi-24 Hind armed helicopters were to act as flying artillery ahead of the main attack force. The Soviets deployed highly mobile bridging equipment with their advance echelons to ensure river obstacles could be quickly crossed and the tempo of advance maintained.

Up to five or six Soviet and Warsaw Pact divisions were grouped in combined armies. These were, in turn, supported by specialist artillery and rocket units to enhance the firepower available during breakthrough operations. According to Soviet doctrine, tactical nuclear and chemical weapons strikes were to be closely integrated with armored attacks to increase demoralization and confusion among the enemy. The widespread availability of NBC protective clothing and decontamination equipment was meant to ensure that Soviet forces could maintain their pace of advance even on a contaminated battlefield. Recently declassified Soviet war plans envisaged more than 2,000 tactical nuclear strikes in western Germany alone during the first 14 days of any Soviet offensive; this would allow the Red Army to reach the Rhine in 14 days and then to push to Spain in a further 20 days. Whether the Soviet plan would have worked is still a matter of great debate, with many analysts believing that global nuclear war would have been initiated before the Red Army could have achieved a conventional victory in Europe. In the 1970s such questions were at the top of the agenda for NATO policy makers. It was decided in the mid-1970s that NATO needed to develop the weapons and doctrine to counter any Soviet *Blitzkrieg*. Armored forces would be central to the rebuilding of NATO's conventional forces over the next decade.

A major contributing factor to a resurgence in the interest in armored warfare in NATO countries was the experience of Israel during the 1967 and 1973 wars. In both those conflicts Israeli tank units roundly defeated Arab armored forces equipped with new Soviet tanks and sent into battle using Soviet armored tactics and doctrine. In the 1967 Six Day War Israeli tank units, with lavish air support, broke through Arab defenses on three fronts and advanced 100 miles or more to the

operations convinced them that a hard-hitting and highly mobile armored force was needed to capitalize on any battlefield success created by nuclear strikes. Nevertheless, the overall size of the ground forces was slashed by Khrushchev in the late 1950s, with their strength dropping by more than half to 1.6 million men. The remaining tank divisions were fully mechanized and new motorized or motor-rifle divisions created. Armored vehicles gave these new formations mobility to prevent them being easily targeted for NATO nuclear strikes. Armored protection was also a means to ensure the soldier could survive on the irradiated battlefield of the future.

The demise of Khrushchev in the early 1960s ensured that the ground forces would regain their pre-eminence in the Soviet armed forces. The next 15 years

Suez Canal. This was a classic *Blitzkrieg* offensive that totally overwhelmed the ability of the Arab armies to recover from the shock of the first Israeli attack and co-ordinate a viable defense.

Six years later, during the Yom Kippur War, the Israelis found themselves on the defensive against a massive Soviet-style offensive. On the Suez Canal, Egyptian bridging units breached the water obstacle in a matter of hours allowing hundreds of tanks to cross. On the Golan Heights, massed Syrian tanks swarmed forward and threatened to overwhelm the small contingent of Israeli tanks guarding the strategic front. In a desperate tank battle Israeli Centurion tanks held off the Syrian T-62s, confirming that superior tank gunnery could be decisive in battle. With the initial Arab advance held, the Israelis went onto the offensive. Poor armor-infantry-artillery co-operation meant that the first Israeli counterattacks were repulsed with heavy losses by Arab infantry armed with wire-guided anti-tank missiles. After they reorganized and learned their lesson, the Israelis attacked and crossed the Suez Canal, trapping a huge Egyptian force.

At almost the same time as the Yom Kippur War was raging, the U.S. Army was beginning the painful task of rebuilding itself after the withdrawal from Vietnam. It established the Training and Doctrine Command (TRADOC) to come up with a new doctrine to enable the U.S. Army to take on and defeat any Soviet *Blitzkrieg*. In 1976 it published Field Manual 100-5 (FM 100-5) which was to revolutionize the U.S. Army's way of war. This subsequently evolved into what became known as AirLand Battle doctrine. Maneuver and firepower, with high technology tanks, armored vehicles, multi-barrel rocket launchers and attack helicopters, were at the center of AirLand Battle to allow U.S. forces to win against more numerous Soviet armored units. Tanks were a key component of AirLand Battle, providing the firepower necessary to defeat any Soviet tank thrust and then the mobility to allow U.S. units to take the offensive.

During the early 1980s U.S. Army units began to receive the equipment designed as a result of this doctrinal shift, such as the M1 Abrams tank, the M2 Bradley Infantry Fighting Vehicle, the Multiple Launch Rocket Systems (MLRS) and the AH-64 Apache attack helicopter. The U.S. Army in Europe became one of the most powerful armored formations in the history of warfare.

In line with their American allies, the British, Germans and French were also developing new armored warfare concepts to counter Soviet armored breakthroughs. The British and Germans also

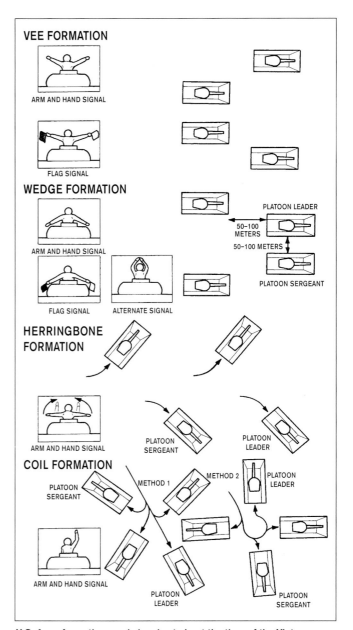

U.S. Army formations and signals at about the time of the Vietnam War.

recognized the pre-eminence of the tank as an anti-armor weapon, developing powerful 120mm guns to equip their tanks. They, however, were keen to use their tanks offensively after blocking forces had brought the first wave of Soviet tanks to a halt. In the Northern Army Group of NATO, which was deployed to defend the North German Plain, plans were developed to use brigades of anti-tank guided-missile-armed airmobile infantry. These were to be "speed bumps" to gain time for the armor to gather and strike at the exposed flanks

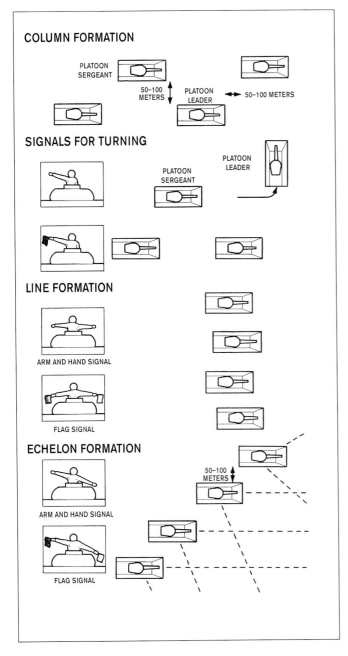

COLUMN FORMATION

PLATOON SERGEANT

50–100 METERS

PLATOON LEADER ←→ 50–100 METERS

SIGNALS FOR TURNING

PLATOON SERGEANT

PLATOON LEADER

LINE FORMATION

ARM AND HAND SIGNAL

FLAG SIGNAL

ECHELON FORMATION

ARM AND HAND SIGNAL

50–100 METERS

FLAG SIGNAL

widespread use of helicopters, armed with anti-tank guided missiles, on both sides in a high intensity armored battle.

For tank crews, from the 1960s through to the late 1980s, gunnery was the key battle-winning skill. With tank guns, such as the British 105mm and German 120mm, now powerful enough to punch through even the toughest enemy tank armor, the tank crew that got off the first accurate round was almost certain to win any engagement. The accuracy of tank gunnery systems was transformed by the 1980s, making first-time hits a realistic achievement. However, this technological revolution was only as good as the training provided to crews and their tactics.

Under the direction of the dynamic General Israel Tal during the 1960s the Israeli Defense Force (IDF) Armored Corps emphasized tank gunnery as the top priority. Tank crews were trained to a high degree in gunnery drills, until they could find targets, lay the gun on target, load rounds and fire in a matter of seconds. Israeli tank commanders were taught to be aggressive and take risks. Finding targets was a high priority and tank commanders normally fought from open turrets, scanning the horizon looking for enemy tanks. Time and again during the Six Day War, Israeli tank commanders were able to get in the first shot, before their Arab opponents, who fought closed down inside their tanks, knew what was happening around them.

When attacked during the Yom Kippur War, Israeli tank gunners proved they were masters of defense. On the Golan Heights the 170 defending Israeli tank crews positioned their tanks hull-down to protect themselves during mass Syrian attacks. From cover, the outnumbered Israelis were able to keep up a furious rate of fire and decimate the attacking phalanx of 1,500 Syrian tanks. Israeli tank crews changed position every minute or so to prevent the Syrians pin-pointing their positions. These movements, known as "jockeying," were carefully choreographed by Israeli tank platoon commanders so that some of their tanks were always firing, while others moved to new fire positions. This meant the Syrians had to face a constant wall of fire. The Israelis were operating from prepared positions or ramparts, called berms, which meant they always had cover for their tanks on key elements of the battlefield. These were built to dominate specific "kill zones" in valleys or roads which restricted the Syrians' movement and prevented them maneuvering against the Israelis. The result was a slaughter. More than 500 Syrian tank hulks littered the battlefield at the end of the first day of the war.

Once the Israelis went over to the offensive they were met by storms of Sagger anti-tank guided missiles and

of the Soviet spearheads. The French also developed mobile warfare concepts and fielded armored divisions equipped with AMX-10 "wheeled tanks" and other armored vehicles to maneuver around the flanks of Soviet armored spearheads.

Again the Israelis provided further impetus to NATO armored warfare developments as a result of their offensive into Lebanon in the summer of 1982. This war saw the first engagements between the new Soviet T-72 and Western-designed tanks. It also saw the first

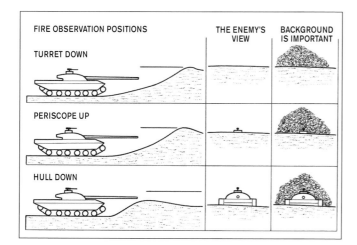

FIRE OBSERVATION POSITIONS | THE ENEMY'S VIEW | BACKGROUND IS IMPORTANT

TURRET DOWN

PERISCOPE UP

HULL DOWN

Rocket Propelled Grenades (RPGs). To neutralize these weapons the Israelis resorted to firing dense smoke screens to blind the missile teams and artillery barrages to force them under cover. This allowed Israeli infantry to close on the enemy trenches and clear a route forward for the armor.

Nine years later in Lebanon, the Israelis used the same tactics to allow their tanks to operate in wooded and urban terrain full of Palestinian and Syrian tank-hunting teams. Even though the IDF eventually fought its way to Beirut, the campaign was long and bloody. There was no dramatic breakthrough, just a series of confused and frightening engagements.

Israeli tanks were restricted to a few narrow valleys and had little chance to operate off-road. The IDF's tank columns were constantly being ambushed by small groups of Syrian tanks, RPG teams or HOT missile armed Gazelle helicopters. What was supposed to be a *Blitzkrieg* rapidly stalled. The once dashing Israeli tanks crews overnight became cautious. Only through working with infantry, air defense gunners and artillery could the momentum of the advance be maintained. The intervention of Syrian anti-tank helicopters was a new and unexpected experience that could paralyse whole Israeli tank battalions. The highly accurate missiles were fired from unexpected directions, and tank crews found it very difficult to locate the helicopters as they popped up from behind hills to fire.

Tank Technology

In the post-World War II period, tank technology developed slowly at first, but during the 1970s and 1980s new sensor, fire control and armor advances totally transformed the nature of armored warfare.

The need to counter the Soviet JS III tank in the immediate post-war period prompted a spate of work to develop new high velocity tank guns. The British led this effort and their 105mm gun eventually became the standard for Western tanks during most of the 1960s and 1970s. Its armor-piercing discarding sabot (APDS) round was able to punch through any known tank armor of the time. This powerful ammunition was supplemented later by a fibn-stabilized version (AFSDS) which was even more effective.

Tank design otherwise stagnated in Western countries during the 1950s and most of the 1960s. The U.S. and British armies concentrated on incremental upgrades to their M46/47/48 and Centurion series tanks, rather than building new designs. Additions included new armor, semi-automatic transmissions, joystick steering controls, new turret designs and stereoscopic range finders. On the Centurion, the British tried to improve gunnery accuracy by installing a co-axial ranging machine gun that fired tracer rounds to allow the gunner to judge ranges.

Revolutionary developments were left to the Russians. Their T-54/55 tank with its low silhouette,

Name: Centurion Mark VII

Designer/Manufacturer: Royal Ordnance Factories and others

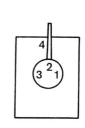

Weight: 51/57.1 tons (51.8 tonnes)

Main armament: 1 x 105mm rifled

Secondary armament: 2 x machine guns

Powerplant: 650hp Rolls-Royce gasoline

Frontal armor: 152mm

Hull length: 25ft 8in (7.82m)

Width: 11ft 2in (3.39m)

Height: 9ft 11in (3.01m)

Speed: 21mph (34km/hr)

Crew: 4

Date entered service: 1959 (Mk I 1945)

Claim to fame: Best British tank ever produced

Above: **Israel up-gunned its Centurions in the early 1970s with 105mm weapons to ensure they remained effective against the new Soviet T-62s being supplied to her Arab enemies after their defeat in the Six Day War. (IDF Spokesman)**

stabilized gun and dome shaped turret set the pace in tank design until the 1970s. In 1961 they followed up the T-54/55 with the T-62, which featured a revolutionary smoothbore 115mm main armament that fired fin-stabilized rounds. The Soviets envisaged their tanks firing on the move to overwhelm defenders by weight of fire rather than relying on well aimed fire from stationary positions. One of the most important features of these tanks was the installation of infra-red night vision systems. The first encounters with these tanks in the 1967 and 1973 Mid-East Wars prompted Western countries to accelerate improvements in their tank armadas.

The U.S. Army had already further improved its M48 Patton tank as the M60 armed with a version of the British 105mm gun. The Army also tried another tactic tried by developing the 152mm Shillelagh gun/missile system for the M60A2, but this weapon and the Sheridan system as a whole were prone to accidents. The M60A2 was prone to catastrophic turret explosions and it soon developed a reputation as a "widow maker," after several crews were killed during

Name: T-55

Designer/Manufacturer: State factories in USSR, Czechoslovakia, Poland and China

Weight: 35.4/39.6 tons (36 tonnes)

Main armament: 1 x 100mm

Secondary armament: 1 x machine gun

Powerplant: 580hp V-12 diesel

Frontal armor: 203mm

Hull length: 21ft 1in (6.45m)

Width: 10ft 9in (3.27m)

Height: 7ft 11in (2.4m)

Speed: 31mph (50km/hr)

Crew: 4

Date entered service: 1960

Claim to fame: Standard Communist Bloc tank of the 1950s and 1960s

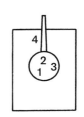

training accidents. Once the Abrams tank entered service there was no longer a need for the Shillelagh's long range killing power. The weapon remained in service until the early 1990s on the M551 Sheridan airportable tank, which saw action in Panama and the Gulf War with the U.S. 82nd Airborne Division.

The Germans were the first Western nation to produce a truly new main battle tank design in the post-war period, with their Leopard, which entered service with the *Bundeswehr* in 1966. The sleek Leopard was the first Western tank purposely designed around the 105mm gun. A year later, the British fielded the first versions of their new Chieftain tank which boasted a 120mm main armament. This fired a new type of round first known as high explosive plastic (HEP), or as the British called it, high explosive squash head (HESH). This round was designed to slam into enemy armor and detonate outside in such a way that hot metal fragments would break off inside the tank, causing catastrophic damage.

While the hardware of Western tanks may have been uninspiring during this period, great advances were being made in fire-control system design because of developments in electronics and computer technology. In response to Soviet active infra-red night vision systems, which could be "seen" by other infra-red systems, the West developed passive night vision devices based firstly on image-intensifiers and then thermal

Name: M26 Pershing

Designer/Manufacturer: Detroit Tank Arsenal, Fisher Body

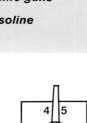

Weight: 41.1/46 tons (41,730kg)

Main armament: 1 x 90mm

Secondary armament: 3 x machine guns

Powerplant: 500hp Ford V-8 gasoline

Armor: 102mm

Hull length: 22ft 4in (6.80m)

Width: 11ft 6in (3.50m)

Height: 9ft 1in (2.76m)

Speed: 30mph (48km/hr)

Crew: 5

Date entered service: 1944

Claim to fame: Most powerful U.S. tank of WWII

Name: M60

**Designer/Manufacturer:
Detroit Tank Arsenal**

**Weight: 51.8/58 tons
(52.6 tonnes)**

**Main armament:
1 x 105mm rifled**

Secondary armament: 2 x machine guns

Powerplant: 750hp Continental V-12 diesel

Armor: 120mm

**Hull length: 22ft 10in
(6.95m)**

Width: 11ft 11in (3.63m)

Height: 10ft 9in (3.27m)

Speed: 30mph (48km/hr)

Crew: 4

Date entered service: 1956

**Claim to fame: Standard
U.S. tank of 1960s and 1970s**

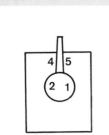

Left: **A Bosnian Serb T-55 tank abandoned on the outskirts of Sarajevo in 1995 after NATO airpower and UN troops forced the Serbs to pull their heavy weapons away from the city. (NATO)**

Below: **The M47 tank and M50 Ontos gun carrier, armed with six 106mm recoilless rifles, were typical of the less than inspiring designs of armored vehicles by the U.S. in the 1950s.**

Bottom: **The M551 Sheridan light tank was developed to provide the U.S. Army with a parachute dropable vehicle for its rapid reaction forces. (Tim Ripley)**

Name: Leopard 1

Designer/Manufacturer: Krauss-Maffei

Weight: 39.4/44.1 tons (40 tonnes)

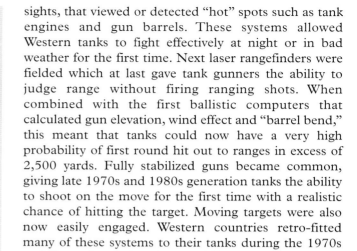

Main armament: 1 x 105mm rifled

Secondary armament: 2 x machine guns

Powerplant: 830hp MTU diesel

Frontal armor: 70mm

Hull length: 23ft 3in (7.09m)

Width: 10ft 8in (3.25m)

Height: 8ft 7in (2.61m)

Speed: 40mph (65km/hr)

Crew: 4

Date entered service: 1965

Claim to fame: First post-war German tank

sights, that viewed or detected "hot" spots such as tank engines and gun barrels. These systems allowed Western tanks to fight effectively at night or in bad weather for the first time. Next laser rangefinders were fielded which at last gave tank gunners the ability to judge range without firing ranging shots. When combined with the first ballistic computers that calculated gun elevation, wind effect and "barrel bend," this meant that tanks could now have a very high probability of first round hit out to ranges in excess of 2,500 yards. Fully stabilized guns became common, giving late 1970s and 1980s generation tanks the ability to shoot on the move for the first time with a realistic chance of hitting the target. Moving targets were also now easily engaged. Western countries retro-fitted many of these systems to their tanks during the 1970s and into the early 1980s, while new vehicles that incorporated them as standard began to roll off the production lines.

The Germans and Americans designed totally new tanks in the late 1970s with their Leopard 2 and M1 Abrams entering frontline service in the early years of the next decade. These tanks benefited from all the latest

Name: Merkava 1

Designer/Manufacturer: Israeli Ordnance Corps

Weight: 59/66 tons (60 tonnes)

Main armament: 1 x 105mm rifled

Secondary armament: 3 x machine guns, 1 x 60mm mortar

Powerplant: 900hp Continental V-12 diesel

Frontal armor: Chobham-derived/not made public

Hull length: 24 ft 5 in (7.45m)

Width: 12ft 2in (3.7m)

Height: 8ft 8in (2.64m)

Speed: 28mph (45km/hr)

Crew: 4

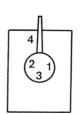

Date entered service: 1979

Claim to fame: First tank produced by Israel

Bottom left: **A Nordic Battalion Leopard 1A4 tank of the Danish Jutland Dragoons on patrol in Bosnia in 1994, where they successfully engaged Bosnian Serb targets on several occasions. (Paul Harris)**

Left: **The Chieftain was the mainstay of the British Army of the Rhine for almost 20 years from 1967 onwards, until the Challenger 1 entered service.**

technology to enable them to fight at night and fire on the move thanks to fully stabilized guns. They also benefited from advances in armor design made in Britain. The Fighting Vehicles Research and Development Establishment (FVRDE) at Chobham developed armor which provided remarkable protective characteristics. This Chobham armor was a composite "sandwich" of ceramics, aluminum, plastic and steel, that absorbed and defeated the hot jets of high explosive anti-tank (HEAT) rounds and tungsten kinetic energy penetrators. It had a distinctive slab-like appearance. The British retro-fitted the armor to their Chieftain, as the Stillbrew Chieftain, and made it available under licence to the U.S. and Germany for use on their new tanks. They in turn further developed the armor and the U.S. Army began to refer to Burlington armor. The first British tank to feature Chobham armor as an integral part of its design was the Challenger 1, which entered production in the early 1980s. The battlefield significance of Chobham armor and its U.S. versions would not be fully appreciated until the 1991 Gulf War.

On the basis of their experience during the Six Day and Yom Kippur Wars the Israelis began their own indigenous research program to field a tank, the Merkava or Chariot, that met their own peculiar requirements. Their number one priority was armored protection so the design was dramatically changed to reflect this requirement. Most strikingly the engine was moved from the rear to the front of the vehicle. The suspension was deliberately hung low to reduce the tank's silhouette, and the main armament was placed low in the turret to reduce this even further. The high rates of fire needed in the Golan battles convinced the Israelis that they needed to increase the ammunition supply their tanks could carry so the Merkava was fitted with a large rear cargo compartment that allows the tank to carry up to 100 main armament rounds, compared to the then average of 50 in Western tanks.

The Israelis were also keen to improve the armored protection of their existing M60 and Centurion tank fleets and designed the revolutionary Blazer reactive or explosive armor. This was basically blocks of plastic explosive fitted around the tank's hull that exploded outwards when a HEAT round impacted, deflecting its hot jet away from the tank's armor.

The Soviets responded to Western tank developments with three distinctive tanks—the T-64, T-72 and T-80. They featured for the first time laminated, reactive and ceramic armor. These armor advances were not apparent at first with Western

Above: **Only when the M1 Abrams entered service in large scale numbers in the early 1980s did the U.S. Army have a tank superior to the latest Soviet or European designs. (Lockheed Martin Solartron)**

Right: **Polish T-72 crews are briefed during a large Warsaw Pact exercise during the 1980s. (Polish Army)**

Name: T-72

Designer/Manufacturer: State factores in USSR

Weight: 44.8/50 tons (45.5 tonnes)

Main armament: 1 x 125mm smoothbore

Secondary armament: 2 x machine guns

Powerplant: 780hp V-46-6 diesel

Frontal armor: 280mm laminated

Hull length: 22ft 10in (6.95m)

Width: 12ft 9 in (3.59m)

Height: 7ft 2in (2.19m)

Speed: 40mph (65km/hr)

Crew: 3

Date entered service: 1971

Claim to fame: Main Soviet tank of 1980s

interest concentrated on the automatic gun-loader that allowed them to operate with three-man crews, though it was discovered that the early versions of this tended to "eat" the arms of the gunner until the glitch was sorted out. The Soviets fitted all three tanks with their new 125mm smoothbore gun that fired fin-stabilized sabot rounds. Later models of the T-72 and T-80 tanks were also able to fire a laser-guided Svir anti-tank missile from the 125mm gun.

The T-64 was the first of the new generation Soviet tanks and appeared in the late 1960s. Its laminated armor was a first for the Red Army and incorporated ceramic material. The tank also boasted armored side skirts to deflect HEAT warheads. Later models of the tank were fitted with reactive armor for increased protection.

The T-72 went into production in the early 1970s and was a far more successful design, because of simpler and more robust automotive components. Its hull and turret were covered in the same laminated

Right: **In time for the 1982 invasion of Lebanon the Israelis had protected many of their Centurions with Blazer reactive armor. This proved effective against rocket-propelled grenades but the tanks proved vulnerable to catastrophic explosions if kinetic energy rounds from tanks penetrated the vehicles. (IDF Spokesman)**

armor as the T-64 but more advanced armor packages were soon added. Known as "Dolly Parton" armor by Western experts, this was fitted around the turret. Then reactive armor was fitted around the hull and turret.

In 1983 the Soviets introduced the T-80 which featured more advanced forms of laminated and reactive armor called Kontakt. This was a multi-layered approach to protection with large armored skirts arrayed around the hull and turret. By layering reactive armor on top of laminated ceramic material it was hoped the new armor would defeat both HEAT and discarding sabot rounds.

The Soviets were not the only ones to look to up-armor their tanks. Iraq for example found its T-55s, T-62s and early model T-72s very vulnerable to hostile fire during its war with Iran and began to experiment with its own versions of Chobham armor. These included laminated armor packs of ceramics, rubber, aluminum and steel. One version included layers of sand inside armored boxes placed around tank hulls and turrets.

These advances were soon countered by Western responses. Firstly the U.S. Army up-gunned its M1 tanks with a 120mm smoothbore weapon to replace its original 105mm rifled gun, and fielded a new improved APFSDS round to go with it. Nicknamed the Silver Bullet, the M829 round was designed to punch through any known tank armor. The British gave their Challengers and Warrior infantry fighting vehicles extra appliqué slabs of Chobham armor. Israeli Merkava tanks were up-gunned to 120mm and Chobham-style armored protection was added. The tank's turret rear was protected by dangling rows of steel chains to detonate any HEAT rounds that were fired into the "shell trap" at the rear of the turret before they impacted on the main armor.

Advances in metallurgy during the 1980s led to the development of new types of rounds and armor based on the waste products of the nuclear industry. Depleted uranium (DU) rounds were designed to replace the tungsten-carbide discarding sabot penetrators that were commonly in use by most armies at this time. Deficiencies in tungsten had long been recognized and penetrators made with it had a tendency to shatter on impact with hardened steel plate, reducing their power. Like tungsten, DU is one of the hardest metals known to man, but crucially it is less brittle than tungsten.

Because of this DU rounds maintain their shape on impact and so have far better penetrating characteristics. As DU rounds penetrate through armor they actually catch fire because of friction effects and on penetration they fill the inside of the target tank with a shower of hot metal fragments. This is usually enough to cause a catastrophic explosion of the target tank's ammunition. Both the British and Americans fielded operational DU 120mm rounds during the mid-1980s. It is believed the Soviets developed a 125mm DU round but they have not publicly displayed this weapon. Israeli 120mm and 105mm tank guns are also believed to have DU rounds available, although the Israelis have kept their existence secret.

So far the U.S. is the only country that is known to have deployed DU armor for its tanks. During the 1980s, a DU armor package was developed for the M1 tank that is supposed to be the equivalent of 1300mm thickness armor against shaped warheads and 600mm armor against APFSDS rounds.

While the race to improve tank guns and armor captured headlines and attention during the Cold War, tank designers also began to pay attention to less glamorous ways to improve the survivability of armored vehicles. It was quickly realized that one of the easiest ways to defeat the anti-tank guided missile threat was to set off smoke screens, so the missile operators would not be able to guide their weapons. Tanks of most armies were equipped with smoke dispensers as standard to allow the rapid firing of smoke screens. Smoke rounds were also provided so tanks could lay down smoke screens on top of missile firing positions to blind the enemy and allow them still to see what was happening on the battlefield.

The next logical step was to fit tanks with active defensive measures to jam or destroy enemy missiles. The Soviets were ahead of the West in this field, developing the Arena system in the late 1980s. This employed a radar to detect an in-bound missile and then fired a Claymore-type warhead made up of numerous small ball bearings into its path to destroy the missile, or fatally damage its guidance system. A small number of T-80s received Arena by the end of the 1980s but the collapse of Soviet defense spending following the withdrawal from Eastern Europe meant it was not deployed with frontline tank units.

The need to operate in a nuclear, chemical and biologically contaminated battlefield meant tanks from the 1950s onwards were fitted with protective equipment as standard. This took the form either of breathing apparatus for individual crew members, or over-pressure systems that turned the crew compartment into a "clean" sanctuary.

Experience in World War II, which was confirmed during the Arab-Israeli Wars, showed that tanks were only destroyed if they suffered a catastrophic explosion or caught fire. One of the principal causes of this was if the main armament rounds, particularly their propellant, caught fire. To counter this deadly threat the internal layout of Cold War tanks underwent considerable change. Main armament rounds were generally stored below the turret ring in fireproof compartments and automatic fire suppression systems installed to extinguish any fires quickly. Electric turret traverse and gun elevation was preferred over flammable hydraulic-fluid based systems. Inert gases could be pumped into the threatened compartments to prevent fires taking hold.

One unfortunate side effect of the dramatic increases in gun size and levels of armored protection was that the weight of tanks increased exponentially. By the 1980s the Western main battle tanks, such as the Abrams, Leopard 2 and Challenger, were in the region of 60 tons, even before appliqué armor kits were fitted. This was on a par with the clumsy German King Tiger of World War II, which had been crucially deficient in having an under-powered engine. Western tanks of the 1980s, however, were provided with some very powerful engines to give them good power-to-weight ratios.

The 62-ton M1 Abrams' gas turbine powerplant produced nearly 1,500 horse-power compared to the 865 horse-power of the fuel-injected diesel engine of the 48-ton M60 tank of the 1970s. Not surprisingly the Abrams has acceleration rates and cross-country cruising speeds far in excess of the M60, even though it is significantly heavier. The Abrams, however, has far greater fuel consumption than its predecessor and its weight means it is unable to cross many bridges safely. When fighting a defensive battle in a narrow sector this is a bearable constraint, but weight has a significant impact on the strategic mobility of units equipped with the Abrams, as was discovered during the 1991 Gulf War.

Throughout the Cold War considerable effort was put into developing anti-tank weapons, as both East and West tried to counter the other's tank fleets. While many pundits predicted that anti-tank guided weapons would make the tank redundant, improvements in armor, such as Chobham-style protection, meant the tank was able to retain its battlefield pre-eminence. These new weapons did not make the tank obsolete but did make the battlefield more complex and increase the level of sophistication of protective systems and tactics that needed to be employed by armored forces.

By far the most significant anti-armor development of the Cold War period was the wire-guided missile, and its close cousin, the laser-guided missile. These guidance systems allowed relatively lightweight missiles to engage tanks accurately at ranges up to 3,000 yards. New advanced HEAT warheads also increased their penetrating power. Missiles like the Soviet AT-3 Sagger, U.S. BGM-71 TOW and European Milan gave infantry units and attack helicopters the ability to engage armor from outside the range of the machine guns that usually provided tank's close defense. However, these were not wonder weapons and they suffered from a number of limitations. The most critical shortcoming was the necessity for the missile operator to guide the missile during the whole of its flight to the target. This could be up to a minute at long ranges, which gave defending tanks the chance to immerse themselves in a smoke screen, or to bring down harassing fire to force the missile operator to abort his attack.

The introduction in the 1980s of laser-guided "fire-and-forget missiles," such as the AGM-114 Hellfire, which used "smart" computer technology to allow the operator to "paint" his target and launch the missile on its way without further guidance, gave anti-tank forces a new advantage.

Mines have long been a threat to the tank and the Cold War saw renewed efforts to increase their effectiveness. On a fast moving battlefield, anti-tank mines lost much of their utility because of the long time it took to lay them and the sheer logistic effort involved in supplying enough mines to create significant obstacles. The great minefields of World War II in Russia and the Western Desert took months to prepare and activate. To get around this problem in the Cold War, both East and West developed automatic mine-laying devices, such as air-launched rockets and plows to seed minefields rapidly.

Indirect artillery and rocket fire were also identified as potential tank killers by NATO because of the need to break-up large Soviet tank formations at long range, before they entered combat with Allied tank units. The U.S. fielded the Copperhead laser-guided artillery round, which was fired from a standard 155mm artillery piece and was then guided to its target by an air

or ground based observer using a laser designator device. Next, HEAT sub-munitions were developed for so-called cargo-rounds. These were designed to be fired by conventional artillery or MLRS launchers; they then dispensed the sub-munitions over a wide area. Because the HEAT sub-munitions were aimed at the thinly armored roofs of tanks they did not have to be as big as weapons aimed at their front or side armor.

The most potent tank killer to emerge during the 1970s and 1980s was the anti-tank helicopter. Early versions were little more than transport machines converted to carry missiles but with the fielding of the purpose designed Bell AH-1 Cobra, Mil Mi-24 Hind and then the AH-64 Apache, the attack helicopter came of age. U.S. and Soviet doctrine envisaged using these machine *en masse* to swamp anti-aircraft defenses and inflict massive losses on tank formations.

One major development during the final decade of the Cold War that had a significant impact on armored warfare in NATO countries, particularly in the U.S. Army, was the development of laser-based weapon simulation equipment. This allowed tank crews for the first time to simulate weapons effects realistically without having to fire live ammunition. Computer devices attached to tanks worked out the type of weapon firing and type of damage it could inflict. The U.S. Army pioneered the widespread use of this equipment at its Fort Irvin National Training Center (NTC). Here whole brigades and divisions of tanks could fight mock battles that realistically simulated weapon effects and the friction of war. Commanders got "killed," ammunition supply vehicles were ambushed and attacking tanks were decimated by anti-tank missiles. Unlike in old style wargames, where participating troops could ignore decisions by umpires that they did not like, at the NTC the technology never lied and the computers immobilized knocked out tanks, no matter how hard commanders tried to explain how brilliant their plan was. This "reality check" was a major factor in the renaissance in the U.S. Army's armored units during the 1980s, leading to requirements for new and better equipment, as well as training a whole generation of tank commanders in the art of armored warfare. The NTC is credited by many U.S. Army officers as the main reason for their relatively easy victory over Iraq in 1991.

Experience of Battle

On the occasions when the Cold War turned into a hot war tanks were usually at the fore front of the action. In Korea, French Indo-China, Hungary and during the 1956 Suez conflict tank forces equipped with mainly legacy vehicles left over from World War II fought in much the same way as they did during that earlier conflict. It was not until the 1960s that new technology and tactics appeared on the world's battlefields. The state of Israel's conflicts with its Arab neighbors proved to be the major testing ground for the latest and best in tank technology.

Six Day War

The 1967 Six Day War saw the Israelis mount a massive pre-emptive strike against their Arab neighbors. Spearheading the offensive was the Israeli Armored Corps of 1,000 Centurion, M48 Patton and up-gunned Sherman tanks. In a series of audacious armored thrusts, the Israelis carved into the 1,500 Egyptian, Jordanian and Syrian tanks arrayed around their borders.

The first Israeli strike was aimed at Egyptian forces in the Gaza strip and Sinai desert. This attack by Lieutenant Colonel Natke Nir's Centurion battalion on the Sinai front provides something of the flavor of the battle. The unit was part of Major General Ariel Sharon's division which was charged with seizing the key Abu Ageila crossroads and neutralizing Egyptian

Far left: **Many NATO armies armed their helicopters with wire-guided missiles, such as the U.S.-made TOW, in a bid to counter the Soviet numerical superiority in tanks on the European central front. (DERA)**

Left: **Laser-based tactical engagement simulation systems revolutionized tank training during the 1980s, allowing crews to practice tactics realistically against "live" simulated enemy troops. (Aerospatiale)**

reserves. An official Israeli Defense Force history of the war details the battle:

"Nir never hesitated at the dreadful odds he faced. Positioning his reconnaissance troop in the lead, he headed his Centurions across the international border into the barren desert. They soon encountered an Egyptian patrol, which fired sporadically—and inaccurately—on the Israeli column before fleeing northwards. Undaunted. Nir's tanks rolled on towards the blocking position. This locality, defended by a two company force, was flanked by impassable sand dunes, and its forward approaches were protected by a dense minefield.

"Splitting his battalion into three companies, the commanding officer ordered one group of tanks into the minefield from the right and another from the left, leaving the third to support the attack, as the battalion's support vehicles had not yet reached the area. However, the combination of mines and increasingly dense

artillery fire rapidly immobilized many of the Centurions, as well as preventing any attempt at repair work. Nir pulled the remaining mobile tanks out of the minefield and reconnoitered with his late-arriving support vehicles behind the sand dunes, all the while planning a new 'set-piece' approach. Using a helicopter, he had a look from above and found a way around the enemy position.

"Nir now moved one company in a wide outflanking drive, bringing them around to the rear; a second company would do its best to engage the position from the right, while the rest of the battalion with air support would mount a frontal attack. Placing his second-in-command in charge of the outflanking company, Nir directed the main attack himself. The air support, arriving right on schedule, rained napalm and rocket fire on the main Egyptian defensive position. Next, the tanks charged in, firing guns and coaxials. Finally, Nir's armored infantry swept into the frontal defense. The tanks swiftly pushed through the blocking position,

Above: **The IDF press-ganged M48 tanks into service to drag the pontoon bridge it used to cross the Suez Canal in 1973 into place. (IDF Spokesman)**

Above right: **Up-gunned Israeli Shermans pass a disabled AMX-13 as they climb up the Golan Heights during the lightning offensive that captured the strategic mountain range from the Syrians in 1967. (IDF Spokesman)**

Right: **Israeli Shermans and M3 half tracks form up for the attack on Rafa during the 1967 Six Day War. (IDF Spokesman)**

wiping out the nearby tank encampment before it had a chance to fire, and leaving the infantry to mop up while Nir reorganized his Centurions for an immediate move onwards, into the Abu Ageila fortifications themselves.

"Near the main road, the tanks encountered heavy fire from well-emplaced Egyptian armor. Ordering counter fire, Nir soon overwhelmed the Egyptian tanks and pressed his forces on in what was now near total darkness. Once more Nir split his troops into three: one task force would block the El Arish axis, while a second held off the eventual approach of the Egyptian 4th Armored Division along the Suez road. Nir himself commanded the main mission, smashing the stronghold of Abu Ageila.

"As Nir's task force rolled towards the intersection it encountered a column of Egyptian forces. Firing point-blank, the Centurions turned the enemy column into a pyrotechnic display of exploding trucks and armored personnel carriers (APCs). The battalion commander then led his group through an Egyptian encampment, firing at anything that moved and creating havoc in their wake. Finally, the Centurions plowed through confused enemy forces to reach the Abu Ageila position itself. In a fierce battle which ensued, Nir was seriously wounded in both legs by an Egyptian shell. Nevertheless, refusing evacuation, he retained command until reinforcements arrived to assist his heavily engaged force." [1]

The famous Israeli 7th Armored Brigade led the attack on Gaza and this account of the action gives some idea of what it was like for the ordinary tank crews plunged into the heart of these battles:

"[General Israel] Tal decided to attack the Jiradi anti-tank position without implementing the division reserve: 7th Armored Brigade's remaining Centurion battalion would attack directly from the road, while the Patton battalion would outflank the enemy from the south. The latter force, led by young Lieutenant Avigdor Kahalani, crawled through the steep sand to within 150 meters of the road. There the battalion encountered a heavy barrage from anti-tank guns, field guns and mortars. Kahalani's tank received a direct hit: the young commander became a living torch. Burning, he stumbled out of the tank, signalling the rest of the battalion not to stop for him, thus exposing themselves. Nevertheless, one Patton stopped and picked Kahalani up. The 23-year old lieutenant was little more than a mass of flames—yet he gave his rescuers a dazzling smile and reassured them: 'Don't worry—it'll be okay.'" [2]

Right: **The U.S. Army developed air and land cooperation during the Vietnam War, with forward air control teams working closely with armored units. This was the origin of the U.S. Army's air-land battle doctrine of the 1970s and 1980s.**

Below: **The Soviet PT-76 amphibious light tank was widely used by Warsaw Pact naval infantry forces, such as Polish Marines, during the Cold War. (Tim Ripley)**

Vietnam

The commitment of American combat forces to the Vietnam War inevitably led to U.S. Army and Marine Corps tanks seeing action. In the first years of the U.S. involvement, senior U.S. military commanders had resisted deploying tanks to Vietnam because of their preference for light airmobile forces. By the time of the 1968 Tet Offensive this view had been reversed and U.S. tanks and other armored vehicles were fighting throughout Vietnam. U.S. commanders found that, except in the mountainous interior and the Mekong delta area, armor gave them good mobility, protection and firepower. When Communist forces launched the Tet Offensive the war became almost a conventional battle rather than a counter-insurgency effort. U.S. armored units were able to move rapidly to contain and then destroy the large Communist units that had infiltrated urban areas, or besieged major U.S. bases. As U.S. concern about casualties mounted and President Richard Nixon moved to pull U.S. troops out of South-East Asia over the next four years, U.S. reliance on armor for protection increased. At the same time the Communists became more ambitious in their military activity, deploying increasing numbers of tanks.

Although there were never large scale tank battles, as in the Mid-East, because U.S. tanks were generally split up into small groups to support infantry units, the experience did much to shape American thinking about air-land operations, particularly the integration of helicopters into the all-arms battle.

At the small unit level, the Vietnam war taught, or re-taught, the U.S. Army a lot of basic skills, as this account of the first fight against Communist tanks illustrates:

"It was at Ben Het in March 1969 that American and North Vietnamese armor clashed for the first and only time. Both Sergeant First Class Hugh H. Havermale and Staff Sergeant Jerry W. Jones of 1st Battalion, 69th Armor, heard the sound of tracks and heavy engines through the noise of the artillery. With no free world tanks to the west, the probability of an enemy tank attack sent everyone into action. High explosive anti-tank (HEAT) ammunition was loaded into the tank guns and from battle stations all eyes strained into the darkness.

"In his tank, Havermale scanned the area with an infrared search light but could not identify targets in the fog. Sergeant Jones, from his tank, could see the area from which the tank sounds were coming but had no search light. Tension grew. Suddenly an anti-tank mine exploded 1,100 meters to the southwest, giving away the location of the enemy: the battle for Ben Het now began in earnest.

"Although immobilized, the enemy PT-76 tank that had hit the mine was still able to fight. Even before the echo of the explosion had died, the PT-76 had fired a round that fell short of the defenders' position. The remainder of the enemy force opened fire, and seven other gun flashes could be seen. The U.S. forces returned the fire with HEAT ammunition from the tanks and fire from all the other weapons as well. Specialist 4 Frank Hembree was the first American tank gunner to fire and he remembers 'I only had his muzzle flashes to sight on, but I couldn't wait for a better target because the shells were landing real close to us.' The muzzle flashes proved to be enough for Hembree: his second round turned the enemy tank into a fire ball.

"Captain Stovall called for illumination from the camp's mortar section and in the light of the flares spotted another PT-76. Unfortunately, the flares also gave the North Vietnamese tanks a clear view of the camp's defenses, and as Stovall was climbing aboard Havermale's tank, an enemy high explosive round hit the loader's hatch. The concussion blew Stovall and Havermale from the tank, and killed the driver and loader. Damage to the tank was slight.

"Jones took charge, dismounted, and ran to another tank which was not able to fire on the enemy's main avenue of approach. Still under hostile fire, he directed the tank to a new firing position where he quickly sighted a PT-76 beside the now burning hulk of the first enemy tank. The gunner, Specialist 4 Eddie Davis, took aim on one of the flashes and fired. 'I wasn't sure of the target,' Davis said. 'But I was glad to see it explode a second later.' Every weapon that could be brought to bear on the enemy was firing. Having exhausted their basic load of HEAT ammunition, the crew were now firing high explosive with concrete-piercing fuses. Gradually, the enemy fire slacked, and it became clear that an enemy infantry assault was not imminent. In the lull, the crews scrambled to replenish their basic load from the ammunition stored in a ditch behind the tanks. Tank rounds were fired at suspected enemy positions, but there was no returned fire. The remainder of the night was quiet: the tension of battle subsided and the wounded were evacuated."[3]

The largest-scale use of armor by the U.S. Army was during the 1970 invasion of Cambodia. This was a large scale strike against Communist supply bases or sanctuaries and involved some 40,000 U.S. and South Vietnamese troops. Spearheading the invasion was Colonel Dunn Starry's, 11th Armored Cavalry, the famous "Blackhorse" Regiment. This unit was then the most powerful armored unit in Vietnam, which combined M48A3 tanks, up-armored M113 armored personnel carriers dubbed Armored Cavalry Vehicles, and a strong contingent of reconnaissance and gunship helicopters. Starry takes up the story of his outfit's strike against the "sanctuaries":

"Late on 3rd May, the 11th Cavalry was ordered to attack north forty kilometers to take the town of Snoul and its important road junction. Route 7, leading north to Snoul through large rubber plantations, was chosen as the axis of advance and by early afternoon on the 4th, the lead tanks had broken out of the jungle and were on the ridge astride the highway. Once on the road, the 2nd Squadron, followed by the 3rd Squadron, raced north at speeds up to sixty five kilometers per hour and reached the three destroyed bridges by mid-afternoon. The cavalry secured the site, placed an armored vehicle launched bridge across the stream, and went on.

"With the regiment now strung out for almost sixty kilometers I decided to consolidate south of the second stream crossing. Through the night, the 2nd and 3rd Squadrons closed on the lead elements, which were now reconnoitering the two remaining crossings. The 11th Cavalry continued north on 5th May after Company H [2nd Battalion 47th Infantry] and Troop G laid another vehicle launched bridge at the second crossing site. The third crossing posed serious problems because it would require a heavy bridge. A flying crane, the CH-54 helicopter, was requested to transport an M4T6 bridge to the site, but by midday when the 2nd Squadron reached the third crossing site the crane pilots and the engineers had made little progress. Anxious not to lose the momentum of the attack, I set out on foot with the section sergeant and the bridge launching vehicle to find a place where the span could be used. After gingerly testing several places, they let down the bridge, tried it out with Troop G, and by 1300 the 2nd and 3rd Squadrons were again rolling north.

"The 2nd Squadron paused south of Snoul to bring up artillery, organize air support, and reconnoiter. Refugees reported that there were many North Vietnamese troops in the town and that the civilians had fled. Scouts from the regimental air cavalry troop had observed heavy anti-aircraft all around the airstrip to the east of the town. In mid-afternoon the 11th Cavalry surrounded the city, with the 2nd Squadron to the east and the 3rd Squadron to the west. As the M48A3 tanks and M113 Armored Cavalry Vehicles rumbled across Snoul airstrip, they were hit by rocket propelled grenades and small arms fire, which ceased abruptly when the tanks replied with canister. After a brisk fight, the anti-aircraft guns were seized. The 3rd Squadron, meanwhile, was moving through the rubber trees to encircle the town, triggering an ambush set to hit the 2nd Squadron. Lieutenant Colonel Bobby Griffin, (commander of the 3rd Squadron) placed artillery fire behind the enemy position, set up gunships to cover the right flank and attacked with I Troop. As the 2nd Squadron moved in from the southeast in a co-ordinated attack, an inexperienced gunship pilot fired rockets into the lead elements. This unfortunate incident caused the gunships to be withdrawn and opened one side of the trap as an escape route for the enemy. The two-squadron attack, however, routed the enemy troops, who fled in small groups in all directions. When the cavalry entered Snoul, the city was deserted."[4]

Elsewhere along the battlefront, combined U.S. Army armor/mechanized infantry task forces were engaged in a series of bloody and confused mopping up operations against North Vietnamese troops who were not able retreat out of the jaws of the American armored and helicopter-borne strike force. Private Harold Spurgeon, of Charlie Company of the 2nd Battalion, 47th Mechanized Infantry took part in one of these actions:

"All of a sudden, guns opened up! Now, it's always a scary feeling when you can't see your lead element but you can hear them shooting. Because now it's a chain reaction: 2-34th Armor opened up with main gun and .50 calibre machine guns. We were about third track behind the last tank, and we're going through thick woods with moss-covered boulders. One tank commander hit one of the big branches and they had to call a dust-off for him. He must have hit pretty fast. I guess you can get hurt that way. They actually had to put him on a stretcher. The tank was parked under a tree, and a big branch was missing, and there was smoke popped. Also, I saw two dead Vietcong or North Vietnamese Army [soldiers] off to the right of the road and one of them—it looked like a tank ran over him. The guy was lying on his back, with his hands out, and his heads and his whole body were rather flat! I figured the 2-34th Armor had some fun going through here. Well, I'm waiting for everyone else to open fire. We see a dead guy, there's got to be a live one around somewhere. And we're riding an APC that's got loads and loads of ammunition. One of the guys starts working the minigun and it lets off one burst—one belch—and that was it. She jammed. The tankers open up

again with 90mm guns. I can't recall any return fire— just our own." [5]

By 1972 U.S. ground forces had been all but withdrawn from South-East Asia, leaving only U.S. airpower to keep the Communist North's army from invading South Vietnam. In the spring of 1972 a huge Communist army struck southwards led by an armada of 600 T-55 and PT-76 tanks. To turn them back the USAF unleashed its newly developed arsenal of "smart" bombs or precision-guided munitions (PGMs). Circling over the battlefield along South Vietnam's northern border in an OV-10 Bronco aircraft was a USAF airborne forward air controller Lieutenant Colonel Ray Stratton:

"I found two tanks just north of [a force of North Vietnamese] on the My Chanh River. It was twilight. There was a PT-76 and a T-54. The PT-76 was trying to pull the T-54 out of a dry stream bed. They were just a mile to the east of [the road] and about a mile and a half north of the town. I called for ordnance and there was none available. I waited and finally 'Schlitz' and 'Raccoon,' two F-4s out of Ubon, showed up. They were equipped with a laser illuminated bomb system known as Paveway One. 'Raccoon' was the 'illuminator,' that is, he carried the laser gun used to direct the laser energy on to the target. 'Schlitz' carried laser guided bombs.

"They checked in with two or three minutes of 'playtime' left—that is they were running short of fuel. I briefed them on the way in to save time. I put smoke down marking the target. By time the [laser] illuminator, 'Raccoon,' was in orbit, he asked me which tank we wanted hit. I suggested the one that was not stuck. Within 30 seconds he said, 'I've started the music,' meaning the laser beam was on the target. 'Schlitz' was already in position to drop—the LGB hit right on the PT-76, blew the turret off and flipped the tank over. The blast covered the second tank with mud, so I put another smoke rocket down. 'Raccoon' 'started the music' again. 'Schlitz' meanwhile had pulled right up the porch for another run. The whole operation was over in three minutes. Two bombs—two tanks destroyed. I logged them in at 6.18 and off at 6.21. That must be a record of some kind." [6]

Left: **Thermal imaging sights revolutionized armed warfare, allowing tanks to "see" and engage targets at night and in bad weather at ranges up to 3,000 yards. (Pilkington Optronics)**

Yom Kippur War

One of the best examples of how the arms race between East and West shaped the nature of tank warfare was the 1973 Arab-Israeli War. The massive defeat of the Arab armies in 1967 led Cairo and Damascus to turn to the Soviet Union for new weapons and advice on how to use them. By now many of the enhancements to Soviet conventional weapons approved by the new regime led by Leonid Brezhnev were beginning to feed through into the equipment and tactics of the Soviet Ground Forces. With Israeli troops occupying the Sinai Peninsula and Golan Heights, the Egyptians and Syrians were very receptive to Soviet offensive doctrine. In particular, the Egyptians wanted assault bridging equipment to cross the Suez Canal and new anti-tank weapons to enable their numerous infantry to withstand Israeli tank attacks. The Syrians, meanwhile, wanted to be able to strike fast and drive the small Israeli garrison back from the Golan before IDF reinforcements could arrive. Likewise, the Israelis had improved their armored forces by up-gunning their M48s and Centurions with 105mm guns and new discarding sabot ammunition. Not surprisingly many observers at the time saw the war as a dress rehearsal for a Soviet attack on NATO.

On October 6 Egyptian troops surged across the Suez Canal, taking the Israeli defenders by surprise. Immediately Israeli commanders activated their contingency reserves to launch local counterattacks to drive back the assault teams and prevent them consolidating their positions. The longer the Egyptians were across the canal, the more likely it was that they could build bridges to start to bring tanks and other heavy equipment across. In the northern sector a company of nine Centurion tanks was ordered to attack. The following extract from an Israeli official history illustrates how the Arab forces had worked to counter the superiority of the IDF's Armored Corps:

"Suddenly, the voice of the commanding officer roused the crews from their half-drowse. 'Alert. Fire coaxial to the right. Bazooka teams.' Nine tank turrets traversed: eighteen pairs of eyes locked onto the sights. The company had reached battle. Slamming a 105mm round into the barrel, the second tank's loader Chuck, waited until the breech clanged shut. He next checked the cartridge belts, making sure the coax was fed securely. Satisfied that all was well, he waited for Yefim to fire. Seconds later, a deafening noise, a suffocating stench and a painfully bright flash assailed the crew as the HESH round left the barrel, to smash into an Egyptian tank-killer team.

"Once more the order 'Follow me' was given and the nine Centurions moved on, reorganising on the road. Scant minutes later, a sudden shriek and then thunder heralded heavy artillery fire. The tank commanders scrambled down from their turrets, slamming the hatches after them. The Egyptian artillery—accurately directed by concealed observers—quickly found its range, covering the area with hundreds of shells. 'Keep moving!' barked the company commander, knowing a mobile tank was a more difficult target. The inexperienced, frightened crewmen, newly inspired by their commander's brisk tone, rallied and took up their tasks with new courage.

"By midnight, the artillery barrage had died down, and the Centurion crews began to relax. The tank commanders, opening their hatches and cautiously peering out, realized the company had reached the Canal. On the company commander's orders, the nine Centurions climbed to hull-down positions, prior to firing on the Egyptians on the other side. As Yefim caught the first glimpse of the scenery in his sight, he shouted 'Stop!' Boaz, the driver, slammed on the brakes, enabling Yefim to open fire from the lowest possible profile. Yaron, the tank commander, traversed the gun sight with his dual control and ordered Yefim to fire an Armor Piercing Discarding Sabot (APDS) round. With split second precision, Chuck loaded the round, the breech clanged shut, and Yefim pressed the firing pedal. Half a mile away, an Egyptian T-55 exploded in a blaze of fireworks.

"The Egyptians at first hard-hit, rallied fast. Infantry teams carrying Sagger anti-tank missiles crept into position along the east bank of the Canal. Egyptian artillery resumed the deadly barrage. Israeli tanks were hit—and so were Egyptian infantrymen, cut down by the artillery assigned to support them. Yaron's tank was hit below the turret by an Egyptian Rocket Propelled Grenade (RPG). Flames immediately blazed from the rear deck. Calmly, the commander stopped his Centurion and ordered fire extinguishing drill. But despite the precision drill, the fire quickly got out of control; the crew, bailing out, was rapidly picked up by another tank. Crowding into the already cramped turret, they did their best to stay out of the way of their rescuers as they loaded and fired.

"Suddenly, a flash of blood-red light enveloped the tank next to the one which had picked up Yaron's crew. The whole front of the turret seemed to melt into a reddish mass of molten steel. As eight men huddled inside the rescuing tank watched horrified, a blazing shape thrust itself out of the commander's hatch and rolled over and over in the sand, trying to extinguish the

flaming overalls it wore. A crewman—the driver— jumped free of the tank; the other two were nowhere to be seen. Then, with a fearsome roar, the tank exploded; flying fragments struck the commander and driver, killing them instantly.

"There was a sudden hush. Then the company [radio] network came alive. 'Stations Gadi, Stations Gadi, over.' Did the company commander's voice tremble? No one was sure. 'Prepare to move out in column, Follow me!' Then the seven remaining Centurions left the killing ground, studded with dozens of Egyptian casualties—and the charred bodies of four of their own comrades—and rolled into the first light of dawn. To the next battle."[7]

On the Golan front Major General Rafael Eitan's two tank brigades were facing a massive Soviet-style tank assault. Within hours his men were fighting for their lives and according to the general, the outcome turned on the quality of a handful of Centurion tanks and their crews:

"Our border on the Golan had no natural obstacles to hinder an assault by the Syrians, but we had constructed 17 strong points, each holding 20 men and three tanks, extensive minefields and a deep, four meter wide anti-tank ditch, partly filled with water. The 7th Brigade with 90 Centurions manned the northern half of the line, while the Barak Brigade with 75 tanks held the southern sector, We hoped the Syrian attack would be blunted by these defenses, which would have to be crossed in the face of accurate fire from our tanks sited behind earth ramparts or in hull down positions.

"The initial Syrian offensive was directed at the southern and central border areas. Our forces were able to contain these early attacks. On the night of 6th/7th October, one company of the 7th Brigade, a unit numbering eight tanks under the command of Captain Meir Zamir, was directed to assist a neighboring reserve south of the town of Kuneitra. The commander of the company arranged the vehicles in such a way as to close the main artery along which the Syrian 43rd Armored Brigade was travelling. In a night battle, at medium and close ranges, the company succeeded in halting and destroying the enemy brigade without suffering any losses. Their actions prevented the collapse of the central sector of the Golan Heights. It was a simple, but effective, example of this heroic and superbly trained tank corps in action. After the Syrian offensive had been beaten off in the southern and central sectors, their effort was concentrated along the northern front. We faced a total of 500 tanks and 700 armored personnel carriers.

The 7th Brigade was deployed to stop this thrust, and the battle fought between Boster Hill and Tel Hermonit, in the area that later became known as the Valley of the Tears, began.

"On Monday morning (the 8th) after a devastating preliminary bombardment, a group of tanks and troop carriers, with support of heavy covering fire from rockets and artillery moved towards the tanks of the 7th Brigade. Our imperturbable artillery-men laid down a barrage on the enemy who were only 400 meters away. But their valiant efforts were not enough to stop the mass of threatening, murderous tanks crawling towards our frontline troops. There were no reinforcements available to us and we could not support the 7th Brigade. Every officer and man of that unit knew that they could expect no help. They would have to rely on their own strength and the superb fighting qualities of the Centurion tank.

"Once the Syrians had forced a way through our minefields, their tanks and supporting infantry converged on the anti-tank ditch. They knew that we had turned all the crossing points into killing grounds, but they were highly motivated and ready to accept heavy casualties. Their MTU bridge-layers were the Centurions' first targets until, one after another, they were knocked out, together with dozens of their escorting T-55s and T-62s. Despite massive losses, the Syrians came on, and such was their courage that infantrymen with entrenching tools succeeded where the bridge-layers had failed: they constructed causeways over the ditch in the face of heavy machine gun fire.

"Ignoring their losses and the obstacles in their path, the Syrians continued to advance in an almost suicidal fashion until their leading tanks were only a few meters from the defenses. From the beginning of the battle, the entire area in which the brigade had been deployed, including deep behind the lines, had been heavily shelled. It was totally impossible to rearm those tanks standing in the firing line, nor could they move to the rear, where the brigade's ammunition depot was located, because any withdrawal would have opened dangerously large gaps in the weakly-held frontline.

"Ammunition was running out and there were no reinforcements to replace our losses, although some isolated tanks did manage to move about 2,000 meters to the rear and gather a few precious shells before returning to the battle line. In some cases our tanks returned to their positions at the same time as the emplacements were being overrun by advancing Syrians. These enemy tanks were destroyed by our tanks still in position swinging their 105mm guns through 180 degrees to fire at the enemy's thinner rear armor. At the

same time, the Syrians were also being engaged by our rearmed comrades returning from the ammunition depot. At such close ranges our guns wrought untold damage on the Syrian hordes. When these intruders had been destroyed our tanks turned their guns forward again, and, from a range of only a few meters were able to destroy the next wave that the enemy threw at us."[8]

Lebanon 1982

In the aftermath of the Yom Kippur War, the IDF Armored Corps underwent a major reorganization to take advantage of the lessons of the encounters with the Arab armies equipped with the latest Soviet weaponry. By the early 1980s Israel was preoccupied with events in the Lebanon. In June 1982 the Israeli army invaded Lebanon with the publicly stated aim of creating a buffer zone against Palestinian "terrorist" attacks against northern Israel. Within days the war had widened, after Israeli Defense Minister Ariel Sharon ordered the IDF to take Beirut, and a full scale war was being waged against Syrian forces in the strategically vital Beka'a valley.

Israeli war correspondents Ze'ev Schiff and Ehud Ya'ari described what happened when Israeli tank crews met Syrian anti-tank helicopters for the first time on June 8, 1982:

"That afternoon a new, unfamiliar weapon made its battlefield debut in a bid to halt Eitan's column—

Below: **Israeli Centurions and Merkavas cover an infantry assault during the invasion of Lebanon. Only good cooperation with infantry prevented greater losses to Palestinian RPG teams. (IDF Spokesman)**

Right: **Destroyed Syrian armor litters a valley in the Lebanon in 1982 after a clash with the new Israeli Merkava tanks. (IDF Spokesman)**

Bottom right: **Islamic Mujahideen guerrillas armed with RPGs inflicted heavy losses on Israeli tank units during the 1982 siege of Beirut in Lebanon.**

French made Gazelle assault helicopters carrying HOT missiles with a range of more than four kilometers (and regarded as the best anti-tank missile available). It was the first time any Arab army had used helicopter gunships against Israeli forces. Even though their performance was still less than high, they gained a distinct momentary advantage just by flustering Israeli tank crews. Ground forces have a hard time dealing with gunships, which can fire off their missiles well beyond the range of a tank or APC's machine gun. Portable anti-aircraft missiles can solve this problem but for the most part the Israeli armored columns were not equipped with them.

"The first Syrian helicopter appeared at 3.30, fired two missiles at the tanks in the lead, and scored a hit on the third in line. As its men, all wounded were being rescued, the Gazelle popped up again, and launched another missile that set the same tank ablaze. Since the road was flanked by a sheer drop on one side and a cliff face on the other, it was quite impossible to bypass the tank."[9]

British journalist Robert Fisk was with the Syrian army the following day as it tried to hold back the Israelis from encircling Beirut:

"Teenage Syrian tank crews were desperately and vainly trying to hold open the only Syrian supply route to the Lebanese capital with tanks so hastily positioned on the mountainside that they did not even have time to throw camouflage nets over their vehicles.

"Now instead of the vanguard we found the pathetic remnants of an armored brigade whose crews were staring in fear at the skies. They concentrated their binoculars, apprehensively searching for Israeli jets, but when they came under fire it was not from the air but from the ground. The first shells seemed to come as a shock to them, whizzing across the peaks from the Israeli tanks in Aazzouniye and exploding on the rocky hillsides to the north. It took the Syrians all of two minutes to return fire, swinging their gun barrels across the highway and shooting back at targets they could not even see.

"To the north, we could see the Israeli shells bursting amid the scree, the sound of the explosions cracking and

echoing down the mountainside. Several rounds landed on a smaller road to the south, on a laneway that led to Aley. When we took this southern road, we were stopped by a Syrian T-54 tank whose crew were arguing among themselves about the source of the Israeli fire. When we reached the opposite ridge above Aley, the cloud came down. The high, bright sun was suddenly obscured by a thick mist that clung to the mountain side. Beneath this canopy—safe from the eyes of Israeli bomber pilots — the Syrians were retreating, pulling as much of their armor and artillery out of the upper Chouf as they could save."[10]

The Syrians may not have been able to take on the Israelis tank for tank, but they had a number of élite paratroop units that were well armed with RPGs and Sagger missiles. When an Israeli tank battalion got lost and advanced into a defensive position at Sultan Yakoub on the evening of June 10, the Syrian paratroopers reacted vigorously and soon had the Israelis trapped. Fortunately for the Israelis their M60s had been up-armored with Blazer reactive armor which absorbed scores of RPG hits without penetration. The beleaguered Israeli tank crews were able to keep fighting under an almost continuous barrage of RPGs. When the Syrian infantry started to inch forward the Israeli battalion commander, Lieutenant Colonel Ira Efroni, a mobilized reservist, was forced to order his men to dash for safety. Schiff and Ya'ari take up the story after some of Efroni's men had made panicked radio calls to divisional headquarters demanding to be rescued:

"'Consider the situation, we have three choices,' Efroni posited coldly, 'to break out of here—the odds of making it are pretty bad—to fight to the last bullet or to surrender.' 'We are not going to surrender!' Misha exclaimed, staring at Efroni in near horror at the very thought. 'Then we'd better get out of here.' Efroni pronounced. The remnants of the battalion would make a dash for it, come what may.

"Eleven battalions of artillery were to create a box of fire around Efroni's vehicles to prevent an armored or infantry assault, but they could not protect the tanks and APCs from being hit by missiles, RPGs or other forms of anti-tank fire. At 8.45am the battalion completed preparations for its perilous journey. The tanks gunned their motors, went into gear and began to tear out of the valley. It would take sixteen minutes for the column to reach its salvation—sixteen minutes under murderous fire. The drivers floored their gas pedals, Israeli shells just meters away from the speeding column, and the mechanized infantry sprayed the sides of the road while the rest of the men hunkered down and prayed silently to be saved. Not all their prayers were answered: four men died and six were wounded in that mad dash for safety, and one tank disappeared somewhere along the way and was never seen or heard from again. No one could say how it was hit, but one of its crewmen subsequently turned up as a POW in Syrian hands; his three comrades are still listed as missing.

"'I'm out,' Efroni shouted in his ear piece at precisely 9.06am. Helicopters descended on the battalion to evacuate the dead and wounded, and the search for the missing tank continued for a while, without success. Seven other abandoned tanks remained behind in the valley. They contained a number of innovations and material classified as secret until then—such as the Arrow [sabot] shells manufactured by the Israeli arms industry and the substance that serves as a protective layer against RPGs and shells with hollow charges. For whatever reason, no special effort was made to evacuate those tanks or at least destroy them, and the next day the Syrians simply towed them off. It was an appropriate coda to the fiasco at Sultan Yakoub."[11]

Meanwhile the Israeli armored spearheads approached Beirut, where Fisk and other Western journalists watched the war intensifying. The joint forces of the Palestinian and Lebanese Shia Amal were giving the Israelis their first experience of serious ground opposition in the advance on Beirut. The Shia militiamen were running on foot into the Israeli gunfire to launch grenades at the Israeli armor, actually moving to within 20 feet of the tanks to open fire at them:

"Some of the Shia fighters had torn off pieces of their shirts and wrapped them around their heads as bands of martyrdom as the Iranian revolutionary guards had begun doing a year before when they staged their first massed attacks against the Iraqis in the Gulf War a thousand miles to the east. When they set fire to one Israeli armored vehicle, the gunmen were emboldened to advance further. The Shia were learning the principles of martyrdom and putting them into practice.

"The crew of an Israeli armored personnel carrier abandoned their vehicle and retreated with the remnants of an infantry company into a smashed school building. Many weeks later Israeli troops in east Beirut told me that Shia gunmen had captured a Centurion tank and its Israeli crew. The prisoners were then shot in the back, they said. Certainly two Israeli tanks could be seen smoldering on the roadside Late the same evening, Shia gunmen wearing those same strips of white material around their forehead drove their captured Israeli armored personnel carrier into Beirut. Its message was simple: the Israelis were not invincible after all."[12]

Cold War—No War

For the tank crews of NATO and the Warsaw Pact the nuclear "balance of terror" meant they never had to put their prowess at armored warfare to the test for real. They were constantly shown off in high profile wargames, which saw hundreds of thousands of men and thousands of tanks maneuvering around Europe but not a single shot was fired in anger. Everyone had their view about what would have happened if the Iron Curtain had been crossed, but for tank crews of both sides the 1970s and 1980s were kept busy with trials of strength and skill. It was a key part of deterrence theory that both sides had to demonstrate their capability as openly as possible.

During the 1970s and 1980s NATO tank crews in Europe were a barometer of the alliance's ability to put up a fight against the numerically superior Warsaw Pact. The state of NATO conventional forces became a *cause célèbre*, both for "hawks" worried that NATO was not doing enough to build up its forces, and for "doves" concerned that conventional weakness would lead automatically to a nuclear escalation. Objective assessments of the quality of NATO forces were hard to come by in this highly charged atmosphere.

One place where NATO tank units could be assessed was in the Canadian Army Trophy (CAT). This annual test of tank gunnery skills saw teams from many NATO armies pitting man and machine against each other. Martin Horseman watched the 1981 CAT:

"The flat crack of 105mm tank guns firing down the battle run slammed across Range 10 at Grafenwoehr as a Leopard 1A4 platoon of Panzerbataillon 294 rolled towards the targets 2,000 meters or so distant on a bare sandy ridge. Among the onlookers well to the rear was a noisy gathering of the battalion's tankies cheering every main gun engagement, the glowing rear ends of the APDS training rounds being plainly visible on their 2–3 second trajectories, as were the tracers in the intervening bursts of machine gun fire from the co-axial armament aimed at infantry-type target arrays. It was the last and vital run along the course of this year's Canadian Army Trophy for tank gunnery competition and for the German team it was going very well. As the three Leopards roared back up the range towards the grandstand at the end of the run, with their tank radio aerials newly sporting the national flag, the team clearly felt that they had registered a trophy-retaining score for the Panzertruppen of the Heer.

"During a battle run platoons were presented with 18 main gun targets to be engaged from static positions or while moving forward in the attack, the targets themselves being either static or moving. The competitors were not to know in advance the locations, distance or number of targets that would be presented for any given engagement. Range to the main gun targets was 600–2,750 meters and the targets were exposed for only 40 seconds each. The crews were also presented with machine gun targets—six groups of 120 simulated infantrymen at ranges out to 1,100 meters, with each group located within a circle of 5 meter radius. The machine gun targets could be engaged only when the tanks were on the move, two advances being made—

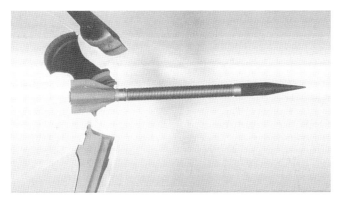

between the starting bound and the intermediate position, and from the later to the final static points. The platoons had 30 main gun rounds for 18 targets and 750 rounds of machine gun for the 60 machine gun silhouettes. The point scoring was based on 500 points per main gun target, with bonus points available for speed of engagement, for successful striking of all the main gun targets and for any unused rounds of main gun ammunition at the end of the battle run." [13]

For the contestants, the event was deadly serious, nation and unit honor were at stake. Promotions were on the line. More importantly, armies partly used the results to justify upgrades to existing tanks or the purchase of new designs on the outcome of the CAT. When U.S. and British tanks came up against newly modernized Leopard 1s in the later 1970s and were badly defeated in the CAT, the bad publicity did much to underpin the accelerated purchase of the M1 Abrams and Challenger tanks. CAT might not have been a real battle but the contest was vital to keeping NATO's armored forces ready for battle.

Above: **The UK's 120mm APFSDS round proved highly effective during the Gulf War. (DERA)**

Left: **Britain's Challenger 2 in action on the test range firing its L30 rifled 120mm main armament, developed from the weapon used to good effect during the Gulf War on the Challenger 1. Laser rangefinders provided tank gunners and commanders with the means to instantly measure the range to a target. This could then be inputted to gunnery computers to adjust the elevation of the tank's main armament to significantly enhance the chance of a first time hit. The major problem with laser rangefinders is that they are what is known as "active" sensors–the enemy is alerted to their tank being "hit" by laser light, allowing them to take countermeasures, such as moving behind cover or firing smoke. (DERA)**

The Battlefield

In November 1989 the people of East Berlin began ripping down the huge wall that divided their city. On orders from Soviet leader Mikhail Gorbachev, Russian forces in East Germany stood by as the country's communist regime collapsed. The Cold War confrontation between the huge tank armies of NATO and the Warsaw Pact was over. In a matter of months the huge armada of Soviet tanks based in Eastern Europe was being loaded on trains and shipped eastward. The unification of Germany then put an official seal on the end of 35 years of east–west confrontation in Europe.

In the summer of 1990 the major problem facing the armies of both the Soviet Union and NATO looked like being how to scrap thousands of their now redundant tanks. There was talk in NATO countries of scaling back their armies to light-infantry-based forces for rapid reaction missions outside Europe. A major conflict involving large land armies seemed a remote possibility. The successful U.S. intervention in Panama in December, where airborne forces, backed by AH-64 attack helicopters, wheeled Light Armored Vehicles and M551 Sheridan air-portable light tanks, had overthrown the government of alleged drug dealer and former CIA agent Manuel Noriega, looked the way forward for Western armies. Then, on August 2, 1990, Iraqi troops invaded Kuwait. Within a few hours they had overwhelmed the small Gulf Emirate. Thousands of Iraqi tanks spearheaded the operation and brushed aside the few dozen Kuwaiti Chieftain tanks that resisted.

Left: **U.S. Army M1A1 in Kuwait during the 1990s. (U.S. DoD/JCC(D))**

Far left: **U.S. Army Abrams tank at speed. (Hans Halberstadt)**

U.S. President George Bush and British Prime Minister Margaret Thatcher decided to offer troops to protect Saudi Arabia and other Gulf countries if the Iraqi dictator Saddam Hussein decided to continue his advance. More than 200,000 U.S. troops were ordered to Saudi Arabia, including a mechanized division and an armored cavalry regiment. Britain dispatched its 7th Armoured Brigade. Diplomacy failed to resolve the crisis so, in November 1990, President Bush ordered the U.S. VII Corps from Germany to move to the Gulf to spearhead an offensive to drive the Iraqis from Kuwait. This was the most powerful armored formation ever sent into battle, with more than 1,200 M1A1 Abrams tanks, 47,000 other vehicles and 120,000 troops. Britain reinforced its contingent to a heavy armored division, France sent a light armored division, Egypt and Syria provided armored divisions and a number of the Gulf states contributed contingents. By the middle of January 1991, more than 4,500 Iraqi tanks were lined up against some 3,500 coalition tanks, for what Saddam Hussein dubbed the "Mother of All Battles." The stage was set for the biggest armored confrontation in history. It involved more tanks than the Battle of Kursk in World War II, but first coalition air forces would be let loose to reduce the combat effectiveness of the Iraqi forces defending Kuwait.

For almost two months thousands of air strikes pounded the Iraqi defenders. The bulk of this effort was concentrated on the frontline defenses, held by poorly led conscript units. Day after day, they were systematically pounded by artillery, Multiple Launch Rocket Systems (MLRS), B-52 Stratofortress bombers, napalm and fuel-air explosives. All these strikes were followed up by leaflet drops offering safe passage to anyone who surrendered. USAF F-111 Aardvark bombers and A-10A Warthogs armed with Paveway laser-guided bombs and Maverick heat-seeking missiles then began to strike systematically at the second echelon of Iraqi tanks, which were being held in reserve to counterattack any coalition breach into the heavily fortified frontier defenses. The F-111s claimed more than 300 hits on armored vehicles and the A-10s accounted for more than 1,000 tanks. Many of these tanks fell victim to coalition airpower when the Iraqi 3rd Armored Division staged a spoiling attack to seize the Saudi border town of Khafji.

By 24th February coalition commander, U.S. Army General Norman Schwarzkopf, judged the Iraqi Army weak enough to be vulnerable to a tank attack. U.S. Marine and Arab units surged forward into Kuwait itself to fix the Iraqi defenders' attention southwards, while the U.S. VII Corps out to the west began a huge outflanking attack to cut off the Iraqis' line of retreat. Its objective was the Iraqi 3rd echelon reserve, the famous armored divisions of the Republican Guard. In turn VII Corps' flank was protected by the XVIII Airborne Corps and the French Daguet Division operating on the far left of the coalition forces.

In four days the Iraqi army defending Kuwait was smashed. VII Corps fought a two-day battle with the

British Challengers during the first Gulf War. Oman has so far been the only export customer for the Vickers Defence Systems Challenger 2. (MoD)

Republican Guard, claiming the destruction of 1,300 tanks and thousands of other vehicles. The British 1st Armoured Division destroyed the Iraqi second echelon armored reserves. For the first time in the history of warfare, senior coalition commanders were able to

JSTARS RADAR IMAGE OF GULF WAR

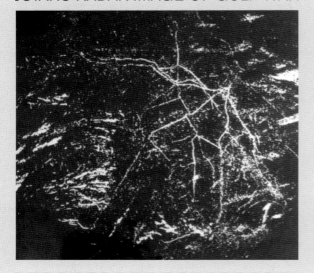

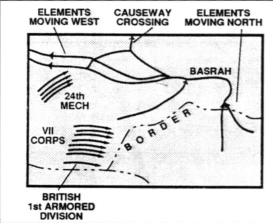

- Lower left, VII Corps in attack on Republican Guards, British 1st Armoured Div in south
- Traffic in KTO moving north out of Kuwait toward Basrah
- Traffic from Basrah moving west on two parallel routes south of Euphrates
- 24th Mech moving to interdict routes
- Upper center, traffic moving north across causeway

watch the progress of the war in "real time," or live, from the safety of their headquarters thanks to electronic down links from ground surveillance radar aircraft, the E-8A Joint Surveillance Target Attack Radar System (JSTARS). This information allowed Apache and MLRS strikes to be directed against Iraqi rear echelons simultaneously as M1A1 tank units engaged frontline Iraqi tanks. At the same time, XVIII Corps hit retreating Iraqi units hard, with tanks and deep strikes by its AH-64 Apache attack helicopter brigades. U.S. Marine and Arab forces also inflicted heavy tank losses on the Iraqis. The U.S. Army's Abrams tank units alone claimed 2,000 kills and U.S. Army Apache battalions claimed 298 tank kills. In return the Iraqi tank crews performed poorly. U.S. tank losses amounted to 18 Abrams written off, but with none having suffered penetrating hits. No British Challengers were knocked out by Iraqi tank fire. The Iraqi Army was devastated, with more than 84,000 men surrendering to coalition forces. The U.S. claimed that the Iraqis lost 3,847 tanks, 1,450 armored personnel carriers and 2,917 artillery pieces. Out of 43 divisions deployed to defend Kuwait only seven managed to escape the American pincer movement.

The Gulf War victory, however, did not set the scene for a decade of peace and harmony, policed by United Nations' forces. The Mid-East, Africa, the Balkans and the former Soviet Union were all scarred by a series of vicious conflicts. Tanks played an important part in the battles being fought out in what became known as the "New World Disorder."

Tanks were center stage in the demise of the Soviet Union, when the Russian President Boris Yeltsin climbed onto a T-80 tank parked outside the Moscow White House to declare his resistance to a hardline Communist coup attempt in June 1991. Three years later Yeltsin called in the Russian Army T-80s to shell the White House, which had now been occupied by another group of hardliners. On the fringes of the old Soviet Union newly independent republics inherited huge arsenals of old Red Army tanks and these vehicles were soon in action in a series of ethnic conflicts that rapidly broke out. Russian intervention in the Caucasus region followed in December 1994, when a large force was sent to crush a Muslim revolt in Chechnya. Ever since, hundreds of Russian tanks have been in action as Moscow's campaign to control the troublesome republic continued throughout the remainder of the decade.

The collapse of Tito's Yugoslavia in 1991 sparked the first of five ethnic wars that devastated much of the Balkan region and sucked in large international peacekeeping forces. Slovenia, Croatia and Bosnia were the first battlegrounds. Yugoslav Federal troops tried to use the large tank forces at Belgrade's disposal to crush the independence movements in Slovenia and Croatia in 1991–92 to little effect. Poor morale, bad terrain and well organized resistance meant the Yugoslav Federal tank forces made little headway. Slovenia quickly secured independence but the war in Croatia became bogged down in ethnic struggle between Croatian and Serb militia forces. Bosnia was smashed apart by a three-way conflict between Serb, Croat and Muslim forces between 1992 and 1995. Except during the Croatian Army advances in the fall of 1995, the frontlines were largely static with little chance for tanks to do much more than act as glorified artillery.

Peacekeeping troops of the UN Protection Force (UNPROFOR) did deploy a handful of Danish Leopard 1A4 tanks that engaged Serb armor on a couple of occasions in 1994. However, it was not until NATO's Implementation Force (IFOR) entered the country to enforce the Dayton Peace Accords, in December 1995, that significant Western tank contingents entered the Balkans. These tanks never had to fire in anger, but did demonstrate the resolve of NATO to enforce peace.

The 1998–99 Kosovo War again saw Yugoslav troops using tanks, this time to crush Albanian rebel forces.

ARMOR IN MALISEVO, KOSOVO

TANK

Above: **NATO air forces had great difficulty finding Yugoslav tanks hidden in the Kosovo countryside during Operation Allied Force in 1999. (NATO)**

Left: **Coalition commanders were able to follow the progress of the land war via radar images broadcast from the USAF JSTARS E-8 aircraft. (U.S. DoD/JCC(D))**

NATO used airpower in March 1999 to try to force the Yugoslav Army and para-military groups to cease their ethnic cleansing campaigns. Learning their lesson from the Iraqis, the Yugoslavs mounted a major effort to hide their tanks in forests, refugee camps, industrial buildings and underground car parks. In spite of tens of thousands of sorties being flown in the following months, NATO bomb damage experts found only 13 wrecked tanks when they entered Kosovo in June 1999. At the same time NATO intelligence counted more than 220 tanks and 300 armored vehicles leaving Kosovo. NATO tanks spearheaded the movement of peacekeeping troops into the Yugoslav province, again to demonstrate the intent of the alliance to enforce the terms of the agreement with Belgrade that ended the war. German Leopard 2 tanks also played a part in the 2001 war in Macedonia, when they were called in to protect the NATO base in Tetovo. During the same conflict the Macedonians wheeled out their vintage T-55s to bombard Albanian guerrilla fighters.

In the Mid-East, conflicts have raged in Lebanon, Iraq, Turkey and Palestine. Tanks have been in the forefront of all these actions. The Iraqi tanks that escaped from Kuwait were pressed into action to crush Kurdish and Shia rebels in the north and south of the country. Turkish troops also relied on armor to spearhead their regular sweeps into northern Iraq to hit Kurdish rebel groups based there. Israeli troops relied on tanks to maintain their tenuous hold on their "security zone" in southern Lebanon until they withdrew in the summer of 2000. When the Palestinian *intifada* resumed in the fall of 2000, Israeli tanks were deployed to besiege Palestinian cities and towns in the Occupied Territories on the West Bank and Gaza Strip.

Throughout the 1990s tanks have therefore found themselves in action in many conflicts. Although there have been few large scale tank battles, many armies found the tank a useful military instruments for a number of reasons. For combatant forces in many conflicts in the Balkans and the Caucasus war zones tanks have been used because they were readily available and offered a way to bombard enemy forces with impunity.

Their sheer physical bulk and noise was useful during peacekeeping and peace-enforcement missions to demonstrate resolve and intimidate local forces. The modern tank's superb night observation systems also made it very useful for surveillance of crisis zones. The heavy armor of 1990s-era tanks also provided superb protection for their crews and reassured politicians worried about the effect of casualties on fickle public opinion. For these reasons tanks have kept their place in most armies' inventories, although NATO countries have scaled back the size of their tank forces by more than half in some cases, as defense budgets fell by up to 45% over the decade. Upgrade programs were launched by many armies to ensure their remaining, but smaller, inventories of tanks remained effective.

Tactical and Doctrinal Development

The end of the Cold War transformed the way armor is employed in the nations of NATO and the armies of the former Warsaw Pact. The tank is no longer seen as being at the forefront of mass armored attacks in the center of Europe. The buzz words during the 1990s were "expeditionary warfare" and "peacekeeping." Tanks had to be able to contribute to the effort by many countries to project power into crisis zones on the fringe of Europe, in Africa or the Mid-East. NATO armies looked at ways to give their armies, and armored units, strategic mobility.

New logistic concepts were developed to support tank units far from home bases. The U.S. began pre-positioning hundreds of tanks in the Mid-East or on ships at the Indian Ocean base of Diego Garcia so they could be rapidly deployed to the region, to be married up with crews flying in from Stateside bases. This was similar in concept to procedures used during the Cold War in Europe. European countries began to develop specialist roll-on, roll-off ferries to move their tank forces rapidly to crisis zones. The British Army even started to use the newly opened Channel Tunnel to move armored vehicles by rail from their bases in Britain direct to Balkan trouble spots. The U.S. Army began to use its giant C-5 Galaxy and C-17 Globemaster airlifters rapidly to deploy small numbers of M1 tanks and Bradley infantry fighting vehicles to strategic locations, in Somalia and Bosnia during peacekeeping efforts for example. This trend culminated in the April 1999 operation when the U.S. Army moved 14 M1A1s by air to Albania to provide ground security for its AH-64A Apache helicopters of Task Force Hawk, which were being deployed to aid the NATO campaign against Yugoslav forces in Kosovo.

During the 1990s Western armies began to absorb the lessons of the massive tank battles of the Gulf War, though not so much because they believed they would have to fight an army with as many tanks as Iraq again. Saddam Hussein lost more than 4,000 tanks and will never be able to put anywhere near that many in the field once more. Only in Korea are Western forces contemplating fighting a battle on anything like the scale of the Gulf War. The main reason for Western governments to fund improvements in their tank fleets

was to maintain their qualitative lead over any potential opponents, so if they ever did have to go into battle they would prevail with minimum casualties. Political leaders in the West seemed now to expect their armed forces to incur no casualties, whatever type of operation they undertook. The only acceptable casualties were zero casualties.

The main lessons of the Gulf War for the world's tank armies were that the current generation of Western Chobham-derived armor now provides excellent protection against any known tank main armament or anti-tank guided weapons, while Soviet-designed tanks proved hopelessly vulnerable to Western tank main armaments. Secondly, Western sensor technology and computerized fire control is now a decisive factor in tank warfare. Whoever can see an opponent first, can get in the first shot. This has the near certainty of causing a penetrating hit against tanks without Chobham-style armor. In the Gulf War Iraqi tanks were being engaged and destroyed without the crews even knowing U.S. or British tanks were anywhere near them.

The tactics and procedures for fighting tank battles almost exclusively by the use of thermal imaging devices, around the clock, in all weathers, caused many rethinks in the Western tank units during and after the Gulf War. Correct target identification proved to be an absolute priority. At 3,000-yard ranges, the limitations of 1990s-era thermal sights meant it was almost impossible to distinguish between types of tank. Correct identification became closely related to good navigation because only by knowing their correct position on the battlefield could coalition tank commanders engage Iraqi armor with any confidence that they were not firing on their comrades. Almost every U.S. and British tank unit was involved in or suffered from so-called "friendly fire" during the Gulf War. Of the 18 Abrams tanks classed as permanent losses, nine were hit by friendly fire. One M1A1 crewman died after a friendly fire hit. The majority of the other losses were caused by mines. No Iraqi 125mm round penetrated depleted uranium front armor of an Abrams tank. Since the U.S. Army's own U.S. 120mm APFSDS rounds were the only ones able to penetrate the armor of Abrams tanks, friendly forces proved more of a hazard to U.S. tank crews than Iraqi T-72 fire.

Most squadron or company commanders were provided with handheld GPS satellite navigation devices so they could monitor their advance across the featureless Iraqi desert at night. In the night battles with the Iraqi Republican Guard, coalition tank units had to keep very strict formation and fire control discipline to ensure they did not inadvertently engage friendly forces. During the battles with the Republican Guard U.S. VII Corps tank units tried to maintain simple line formations, facing directly at the enemy. This prevented confusion and ensured that maximum firepower was brought to bear on the Iraqis. Company and battalion commanders accepted long pauses between engagements to ensure proper target identification and issuing of precise fire control orders, rather than risk any mistakes. As crew's confidence in the quality of the armored protection improved, the disjointed and laborious nature of the target identification process became accepted.

The 24-hour nature of battle during the Gulf War meant that a key element in maintaining the momentum of the advance was the rapid replenishment of fuel and ammunition. Huge logistic convoys were moved close behind the tank forces so they could refuel and rearm as quickly as possible.

Although the Gulf War was mercifully brief, it did provide some lessons on how to counteract the thermal imaging systems used by modern precision-guided munitions, as used by tanks, aircraft and attack helicopters. Thermal imaging devices detect changes in temperature between people or vehicles and the background terrain. The Iraqis found that the best way to avoid being bombed by coalition aircraft using Paveway laser-guided bombs or Maverick missiles, directed by thermal sights, was simply to park up their tanks and never switch the engines on. This is how many of the Republican Guard tanks survived detection and destruction during the air phase of the Gulf War. However, this did mean they were caught by surprise by the rapid advance of the U.S. VII Corps and many Iraqi tank crews were out of their vehicles when the coalition forces started to engage them.

Above left: **USAF C-17 Globemasters are able to carry a single Abrams tank to trouble spots around the world. (Boeing)**

Top: **Even in 2000 old habits die hard. This M1A2 tank barrel was pointed towards Serbia from Kosovo, where it was on duty with the U.S. Army. (Tim Ripley)**

Above: **U.S. Army M1A2 Abrams were sent to the border of Serbia in 2000 to use their superior night vision systems to monitor for hostile guerrilla activity. (Tim Ripley)**

Left: **U.S. Army troops on peacekeeping missions in the Balkans have been provided with lavish Abrams support to ensure they have necessary "force protection." (NATO)**

Below right: **The U.S. Army regularly deployed M1A1 tanks to Kuwait during the 1990s to counter build-ups of Iraqi troops along the border of the Emirate. (U.S. DoD/JCC(D))**

This was not a problem for the Yugoslavs in the 1999 Kosovo War, when Western political leaders publicly declared that they would not use ground forces. The Yugoslav Army was able to disperse its tanks around the countryside. They parked up their armor to make it more difficult for thermal sights to detect it. Decoy plastic tanks, made of sheet and wood, appeared all over Kosovo and were heated by gas fires to deceive NATO thermal sights.

The 1990s have seen Western tank forces engaged in a plethora of peacekeeping or peace-enforcing missions around the world. Tank units have been drawn into these operations for what are euphemistically termed "force protection" reasons. The humiliation of UN peacekeeping forces in the former Yugoslavia, Somalia and Rwanda in the early part of the decade convinced many governments that peacekeeping forces must be "robust" if they are to gain the respect of local populations or warring factions. An effective way to do this was to attach large numbers of tanks to peacekeeping forces and parade them prominently around the theater of operations.

When NATO peacekeeping forces deployed into Bosnia in 1995 and into Kosovo in 1999, tanks were placed at the front of all allied troop columns. First impressions count. Once these operations settled into a routine, tanks were used in a variety of ways to impress upon the local population that NATO forces meant business. A 60-ton main battle tank makes a superb road-block or vehicle check-point. It has the benefit of providing bullet-proof protection for the soldiers manning the check-point if it comes under fire, and it

can return fire in a devastating manner. The tank's power supply also provides constant radio communications and conveniently brews cups of coffee around the clock to maintain morale in bad weather. In both Kosovo and Bosnia, NATO tanks have been used commonly as observation posts around tension zones because of their superb thermal imaging systems. Infantry thermal sights have limited range and power supplies, whereas tanks can keep their observation systems running 24 hours a day.

For low-tech armies in the Balkans or Caucasus, tanks have been decisive in small scale engagements. These bloody "ethnic conflicts" have a distinctive character that runs counter to conventional military logic. They involve small communities arming themselves from a variety of sources, such as disbanding government army arsenals or international black market arms salesmen. These militia forces generally prove to be skilled and tenacious defensive fighters on their home turf. They are, however, generally unwilling to fight and suffer casualties away from home. In such circumstances, mass tank battles are rare. Tanks tend to be used as static pill-boxes in defensive battles but they do provide the key element of offensive operations. Their armor and mobile firepower is often the decisive factor in motivating militia or paramilitary troops to advance out of their trenches towards the enemy. During the Bosnian Serb seizure of Srebrenica in July 1995, less than half a dozen tanks were involved in the offensive but their shock impact on the poorly armed Bosnians and Dutch UN troops defending the safe area turned the battle in General Ratko Mladic's favor. Once the

Name: M1A1

Designer/Manufacturer: General Dynamics Land Systems

Weight: 62.2/69.7 tons (63.3 tonnes)

Main armament: 120mm smoothbore

Secondary armament: 2 x machine guns

Powerplant: 1500hp Lycoming gas turbine

Frontal armor: Chobham-derived/not made public

Hull length: 31ft 0in (7.92m)

Width: 12ft 0in (3.65m)

Height: 7ft 9in (2.37m)

Speed: 45mph (72km/hr)

Crew: 4

Date entered service: 1987 (M1 Abrams 1982)

Claim to fame: Main U.S. Army battle tank of 1990s

Bosnian Serb tanks had crushed the few frontline trenches, the defenders fled and Mladic's infantry could safely advance into the enclave.

Tank Technology

In the aftermath of the Gulf War, Western armies launched a number of programs to upgrade and improve their inventories of tanks. At the same time existing programs to develop new tanks, such as the British Challenger 2 and French Leclerc, continued because of the large investment that had already been made. Other new tank projects around the world fell foul of the global collapse of defense spending, however.

Only limited numbers of upgrades, to a few hundred vehicles, were authorized by hard pressed finance ministries because it was difficult for armies to justify new tank programs when there seemed to be little threat to the supremacy of Western tanks. Only some 790 M1A1s are being upgraded to M1A2 standard by the U.S. Army, the British bought just under 400 Challenger 2s, some 658 Leclercs were ordered by France and the United Arab Emirates and only a fraction of the German Leopard 2 fleet was budgeted for upgrade to the A5 standard, some 225 vehicles.

Indeed the very success of Western tank designs in the Gulf War made people wonder if anything better

General Dynamics Land Systems' Abrams has been the standard tank of the U.S. Army since the early 1980s and it has been exported to Egypt, Kuwait and Saudi Arabia. (STRICOM)

was really needed when the old Soviet tank industry was bankrupt and not producing any more new designs. The poor performance of the T-72 in the Gulf War and the vulnerability of the T-80 during the Chechnya fighting further contributed to the feeling that little needed to be done to improve Western tanks. Without a real and immediate threat there seemed little urgency to spend scarce defense money countering non-existent threats. The main stimulus for upgrading Western tanks came from the need to maintain what became known as the "defense industrial base." Companies such as General Dynamics, Vickers Defence Systems, GIAT Industries and Krauss-Maffei Wegmann needed to be kept in business if the West was to have the option of building replacement tanks at some point in the future, if a new threat did emerge. A number of export orders were also still possible for existing products in the medium term if these companies continued to operate. Lobbying from industry helped a great deal in opening the purse strings of defense ministries around NATO, as governments sought to soften the blow of the defense industry meltdown on unemployment in politically sensitive regions. "Pork barrel" politics undoubtedly

played a part in securing work for the West's tank factories during the lean 1990s.

The Leclerc and the Challenger 2 were the last "new" designs to enter production during the 1990s even through development had started in the previous decade. They both featured improved thermal-imaging and fire-control systems. The Challenger had two thermal sights and laser rangefinders to give it what was termed "hunter-killer" capability. This gave the commander, independent of the gunner, the ability to look for and designate targets. Upgraded M1A2 Abrams and German Leopard 2 tanks were also given this capability. These tanks were the first to field new digital communications and navigation systems. This so-called "tactical internet" allowed tanks in the same company or battalion to exchange information in real-time through data-links, including fire support requests to supporting artillery batteries and handing off target co-ordinates to other tanks. They also boasted in-bedded GPS navigational

Below: **Vickers Defence Systems has developed the Challenger 2E specifically for export customers. It features a new engine, improved observation and battle-management systems. (Vickers Defence Systems)**

Name: Challenger 1

Designer/Manufacturer: Royal Ordnance Factory and Vickers Defence Systems

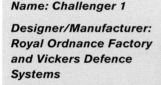

Weight: 61/68.3 tons (62 tonnes)

Main armament: 1 x 120mm rifled

Secondary armament: 2 x machine guns

Powerplant: 1,200hp V-12 diesel

Frontal armor: Chobham/not made public

Hull length: 26ft 3in (8.33m)

Width: 11ft 7in (3.52m)

Height: 8ft 3in (2.49m)

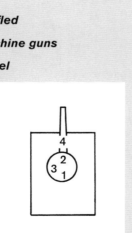

Speed: 35mph (57km/hr)

Crew: 4

Date entered service: 1983

Claim to fame: Main British tank of the 1980s and 1990s

devices. Fielding these systems was seen as the main way to prevent "friendly fire" incidents rather than the alternative of installing electronic beacons or lights. Having a real-time tactical internet that allowed every tank commander in a unit to see the same battle picture was considered a far better tool to achieve battlefield "situational awareness" and prevent friendly fire. While a limited number of tanks had these systems by the end of the 1990s, they had yet to migrate to other vehicles, reducing their universality and hence utility. The U.S. Army conducted large scale exercises for its Force XXI "digitized battlefield" technology in 1997 and has since designated a brigade as a test-bed for the computer hardware and software needed to make the tactical internet an army-wide reality.

Not surprisingly, given the "zero-casualty mentality" of Western governments, the easiest thing to secure funding for was "survivability" upgrades. Improvements to armor, sensors, crew fire protection and new defensive systems attracted the bulk of tank improvement budgets rather than firepower.

Chobham-derived composite armor has been developed even further with the French Leclerc and

Above: **The French Leclerc–this one is *Sgt. Rivoalen* of 3rd Squadron 503 RRC seen during EuroSatory in 1998.**

Name: Leclerc

Designer/Manufacturer: GIAT Industries

Weight: 53.6/60 tons (54.5 tonnes)

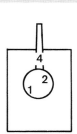

Main armament: 1 x 120mm smoothbore

Secondary armament: 2 x machine guns

Powerplant: 1,500hp V-8 diesel

Frontal armor: not made public

Hull length: 22ft 7 in (6.88m)

Width: 12ft 2in (3.71m)

Height: 8ft 1in (2.46m)

Speed: 47mph (75km/hr)

Crew: 3

Date entered service: 1992

Claim to fame: Standard French tank of the 1990s

German Leopard 2A5s having modular armor packages to allow for new "blocks" of armor to be placed on the vehicle as new designs are developed. The Leopard A5 has been provided with what is termed a "spall liner" in the turret which is supposed to reduce the number of highly dangerous metal fragments that break off inside the tank when its armor is hit by a high velocity round. Not surprisingly the Swedish version of the Leopard 2A5 features even more survivability upgrades, including front and hull side spall liners and improved roof armor to protect against "top-attack" bomblet weapons,

The Swedes also looked to fitting their tanks with a defensive aid suite (DAS) to defeat a range of battlefield threats. Following in the footsteps of the Russian Arena DAS developed in the late 1980s, many countries have been looking at adding this technology to their tanks. DAS systems on tanks mirror many devices used by fighter aircraft and helicopter gunships to defeat missile threats. The U.S. funded the Small Low-Cost Interceptor Device (SLID) program in 1995 to develop an anti-missile missile to counter enemy guided weapons. Radar or infra-red guidance systems allow the SLID to home in on the in-bound missile to destroy it at a safe distance from the friendly tank. The U.S. Army is also looking at so-called barricade decoys that fire ball bearings in the path of an in-bound missile. Central to any DAS system are warning devices, either radars or laser detectors, laser and radio jammers and a computerized control system to activate the system. Except for a small number of Arena systems, no complete DAS had been fitted to an in-service tank by the end of the 1990s. A number of countries have pressed ahead with fielding laser detection devices on their tanks to provide early warning of when they were being "painted" by laser rangefinders or missile targeting systems. There was also widespread use of new "multi-spectrum obscurants" or smart smoke screens, which confuse thermal sights as well as the naked eye by firing a screen of small metal strips around a tank.

Tank firepower developments during the 1990s have been dogged by cost cutting in Western countries. Britain, France, Germany and the U.S. have all standardized their tank main armaments at 120mm and tungsten-sabot rounds continue to be the main anti-armor projectile. Western armies have expressed some concern at the development of so-called "Kontakt-5" and its successor, "Kaktus," explosive reactive armor by the Russians. Its manufacturers, NII Stali, claim it is proof against all the main Western HEAT rounds and depletes the effectiveness of

tungsten sabot rounds by up to 67%, and maybe even be proof against American and British depleted uranium (DU) rounds. The existence of this armor is the main reason the American and British armies have retained their DU ammunition in spite of political controversy surrounding the adverse side effects of this type of weapon on human health. Programs are also underway in many countries to develop new sabot rounds, although for obvious reasons these programs are shrouded in secrecy. So far the Russians have not widely fielded the new armor on their own tanks or exported it, so Western armies have not felt the need to invest in costly new ammunition production.

Battlefield threats to tanks have continued to increase during the 1990s, with new systems, such as

fire-and-forget anti-tank guided missiles and "smart" top-attack munitions, entering serial production around the world. They did not, however, see action during the decade. Legacy programs left over from the Cold War, such as the Sense and Destroy Armor (SADARM) 155mm artillery round, entered service. This is designed to replace the "dumb" rounds developed in the 1980s. "Smart" millimetric-radar and infra-red sensors guide the HEAT sub-munitions towards the weak top armor of enemy tanks.

Top attack technology was fielded in the U.S. Army's Javelin lightweight anti-armor weapon. The "smart"

Above: **The Franco-Swedish BONUS "smart" 120mm mortar round dispenses sub-munitions that are guided to their targets by heat-seeking and millimetric radar sensors. (Celcius)**

Right: **When NATO troops moved into Kosovo, British Challenger 1s were the first allied tanks to cross the border to secure the province for peacekeeping operations. (LAND Command/Kevin Capon)**

missile is programmed to fly over the target tank and fire its warhead down onto the target. In most armies wire-guided anti-tank missiles have been replaced by laser-guided weapons. This gives them a fire-and-forget capability, reducing the vulnerability of the operator.

The U.S. Army's major investment in anti-armor systems was directed towards improving its inventory of AH-64 Apache attack helicopters. They were improved by the installation of a millimetric radar mounted above the rotor blades. The millimetric radar produces a "picture" similar to a thermal sight and allows the crew to differentiate between types of tanks. The Apache's Hellfire missiles have also been modified to be guided by the millimetric radar, reducing their dependence on laser guidance which can be degraded by bad weather or enemy counter-measures. Britain, the Netherlands, Singapore and Israel have all decided to buy the D-model Apaches.

These advanced anti-armor weapons never saw action during the 1990s, however, nor were the advanced tanks of Western armies given the chance to prove their new capabilities in battle.

Experience of Battle

For two months in early 1991 more than 7,000 tanks joined battle in the deserts of Kuwait and Iraq. The "Mother of All Tank Battles" saw the latest in tank technology from both East and West tested in the most demanding combat conditions. For the British and American tank crews it allowed them to put the skills and tactics learned during more than a decade of large-scale NATO exercises in Germany into action in a real battle. They emerged victorious and the West's tank builders found their designs vindicated. The majority of Iraq's tank crews either ended up dead or prisoners because their Soviet tanks were totally outclassed in terms of armored protection, firepower and observation equipment. Saddam Hussein's faulty passive defensive strategy worked in the coalition's favor, allowing coalition airpower two months to work over Iraq's armor with impunity.

Coalition armor crossed the border into Iraq on 24th February 1991. After easily breaching the Iraqi border defenses, American and British tanks spent two days driving across the desert to engage the Iraqi armored reserves. The British 4th Armoured Brigade found the second echelon armored reserves during the morning of February 26. The brigade's armored regiment, the 14th/20th King Hussars spearheaded its advance. An officer serving in its battlegroup headquarters, described the scene as it engaged its first Iraqi tanks:

"We desperately sought to confirm with Brigade Headquarters that there were no friendly forces to our front and that B Squadron, moving forward right of the Battlegroup axis, was clear to engage. As the okay came through, everyone who could climbed up on top of the vehicles to wait for the first round to be fired in anger.

A shout went up as the trace of a HESH round curved through the sky and ended with a brilliant white flash— a hit!"[1]

The officer commanding the regiment's B Squadron, Major A.R.D. Shirreff, led his troops forward to engage an Iraqi tank company and brigade headquarters in a flank attack:

"At 0415 hours contact was made by [Challenger 1 tank] callsign 42 commanded by Corporal Adesile on the right. He reported a large articulated lorry [truck and semitrailer] to his front. This was rapidly engaged and destroyed with one round of APFSDS. From the dramatic fireball that followed, we assumed this was carrying ammunition. Soon afterwards, we had multiple contacts of tank turrets dug in to our front. I ordered squadron line to be formed and all tanks were quickly into action. We contacted the bulk of a tank company to our front and soon there were several T-55s burning. The ammunition on board them continued to explode as the fires took hold inside. Several enemy tanks returned fire but fortunately no Challengers were hit; meanwhile B Squadron took on the bulk of the tank company on the right. A Squadron and the Queen's Company cleared the position on our left which also included a number of T-55s.

"At first light, we had a clearer view of our night's work: burning tank hulks and debris of battle littered the

desert. *Disconsolate groups of Iraqis wandered about in a daze looking for someone to accept their surrender. At about 0700hrs the commander of the 52nd Iraqi Tank Brigade surrendered to Captain Joynson, together with a large number of other Iraqis, presumably his brigade staff. After the war, the squadron leader returned to the battlefield with a regimental expedition. A total of five T-55s destroyed by B Squadron using both APFSDS and HESH were found. All were dug in facing south and most died with their guns traversed right, as they faced the sudden, and deadly, threat poised to their right flank. A few had been destroyed as they attempted to reverse out of their tank scrapes. Seldom can the dangers of digging tanks in as mobile pill boxes have been more graphically illustrated.*

"Thereafter B Squadron crossed the oil pipeline obstacle and went firm in a bridgehead about 3,000

Above right: **The UK's 120mm APFSDS projectile is a two unit round, with the sabot and penetrator separate from the propellant. This aids safety by allowing the propellant to be stored in fireproof compartments. (Tim Ripley)**

Right: **British Challenger Armoured Repair & Recovery Vehicles (CHARRV), seen here during the Gulf War, are typical of the support vehicles needed to keep tank units up and running. (Vickers Defence Systems)**

Below: **British Challenger 1 tanks proved themselves in battle during the 1991 Gulf War, destroying hundreds of Iraqi tanks and armored vehicles for no loss. (Vickers Defence Systems)**

meters plus of the pipeline, while D Squadron crossed and shook out on our right, While this was happening, we contracted a tank company to our front and engaged and destroyed at least 5 T-55s using TOGS [Thermal Imaging and Observation Sight]. We could see, and hear, D Squadron on our right doing the same. Having destroyed the enemy to our front, we moved in troop line up to the limit of exploitation in what was almost a classic squadron advance to contact. We moved bound, made contact, formed line and engaged the enemy to our front. Once they were destroyed, we moved on again, the enemy were contacted, whereupon the same process was repeated.

"Although we contacted, engaged and destroyed a considerable quantity of enemy armor on Objective Tungsten, we were faced with almost no opposition. Enemy encountered were two tank companies, a D-20 howitzer battery, a mechanized infantry company and a logistic installation. Several vehicles were engaged while withdrawing and we believe the bulk of the armored fighting vehicles engaged were empty with crews hiding until the storm of fire had passed and they could find someone to accept their surrender."[2]

VII Corps Strikes

The U.S. Army's VII Corps took two days to race across the Iraqi desert to engage the Iraqi Republican Guard Forces Command (RGFC) armored reserves. Bringing the huge armor formations of the U.S. Army's strike force into action was a complex and confusing business for its commanders, many of whom had obviously not seen action before. Colonel Gregory Fontenot, commander of a task force of the 1st Infantry Division (Mechanized) formed around the 2nd Battalion, 34th Armor Regiment, "The Dreadnoughts," found that, just as he was about to take on the Republican Guard's *Tawakalma* Division in the so-called Battle of Norfolk, two of his companies or all-arms company teams had gotten lost in the darkness.

"Charlie and Delta [combat team] *turned around but still could not see the rest of the task force. To orient them, I launched a star cluster, which drew Iraqi fire but also attracted the mis-orientated, chastened and still missing company teams. As Charlie and Delta passed the command group closing on Bravo [company team's] left rear, they encountered infantrymen in spider holes who wanted to fight. [Captain Tom] Burns, leading his [Charlie] company team back into the fight, discovered a rocket-propelled grenade (RPG) team to his direct front. He announced he would run them down and not fire, since that would endanger Bravo. I told Burns, who was passing to my direct front, to engage them with machine guns. Bravo buttoned up and Charlie team went to work. Burns attempted to run over one Iraqi soldier while a Bradley to his rear scrubbed other infantrymen off his backside. Burns missed his man, who rose and shouldered an RPG, but one of Charlie Team's Bradleys killed the would-be tank killer with a burst of 25mm [Bushmaster cannons].*

"From 0130 until 0430 the night settled into a desperate rhythm of targets reported and divided among the teams, followed by volleys of tank rounds, Bushmasters or TOW [wire guided] missiles where appropriate. In the first hours, the tank force destroyed 35 armored vehicles, 10 trucks and an unknown number of dismounted men and captured 100 Iraqi troops. The enemy seemed to be arrayed in company sized positions, with dismounted company positions*

Above: **British armor laagering during the Gulf War. (MoD)**

Right: **British Challenger tanks were fitted with bulldozer blades to clear lanes through Iraqi minefields and collapse enemy bunkers. (MoD)**

between the belts. In fact, the Dreadnoughts were
attacking down the flank of a reinforced tank battalion.

"Enemy vehicles began to explode and burn with
great violence. Learning from passing their burning
hulks that virtually all of the targets were destroyed
tanks, explained why the Bushmasters had been
relatively ineffective. At one point, Delta Team had
banged away for nearly 30 minutes at six or more
targets believing they were BMP [infantry fighting
vehicles]. Delta Team ultimately destroyed all of them
with a combination of 25mm and tank fire and
discovered, as they passed, that all six targets were
tanks.

"Several of the targets were cold. Believing they were
destroyed by the USAF, I ordered them by-passed. One
of the scouts, forward on the right flank, entered the net

Above: **U.S. Army Abrams tanks were fitted with bulldozer blades to
clear lanes through Iraqi minefields and collapse enemy bunkers. (U.S.
DoD/JCC(D))**

Left: **A sabot round hit on an Iraqi T-72. (U.S. DoD/JCC(D))**

Below: **U.S. Army Abrams advance to engage the Iraqi Republican
Guard. (U.S. DoD/JCC(D))**

to report that he could see people trying to man those very vehicles from nearby bunkers. From that time on, the Dreadnoughts fired on cold and hot targets.

"Once a group of targets were spotted and confirmed, the battalion would stop on line (about 1,500 to 2,000 meters), and engage on the orders of the Team Commanders. Once all of the targets were destroyed the battalion then again moved out on line (usually about 2,000 meters) to the next firing line.

"This system worked but had serious flaws, Since Charlie served as base team, Burns co-ordinated movement that took him off his net, often when his subordinates needed him. To prevent fratricide, team commanders had to clear all fires, which took time. Finally, distributing fires also consumed time. All of these things reduced the speed of the attack to a crawl, during which each soldier believed surely the Iraqis would kill him.

"To add to that frustration, an unexpected phenomenon also occurred at intervals during the night. Several targets were struck, glowed and cooled without even exploding, Again, I concluded these were victims of the USAF. However, the next morning Lieutenant Colonel Daniel Magee, 1st Brigade Executive Officer, found dead crews in several tanks that had neither exploded or burned, which did show sabot holes. Some were probably killed by the Dreadnoughts, but not all of them since the Dreadnoughts, believing they were fighting T-55s and BMPs, fired relatively few of their 'Silver Bullets.' All but a handful of the 40 tanks destroyed that night turned out to be T-72s. The Dreadnoughts did change ammunition after confirming the presence of T-72s, but that occurred fairly late in the battle. The good news is that 120mm high explosive anti-tank rounds do just fine against T-72s. Who or what killed the tanks that did not explode cannot be determined with any certainty. After 0330 the enemy thinned out. By about 0430, the task force had destroyed another 17 armored vehicles. After 0430 the task force encountered relatively few enemy, reaching the limit of advance at 0600 destroying another two tanks and four tracked vehicles. What a night! The good news was the brigade was in reserve. At last, rest and the opportunity to refuel and rearm.

"The fight for Norfolk was one-sided, as the paucity of the Iraqi return fire demonstrated. The Dreadnoughts fired 115 tank-killing rounds but reported only a dozen or so returned rounds. Firing in platoon volleys also proved effective. The benefit of volley fire on multiple targets is shock and suppression of the enemy. On more than one occasion during that long night in February 1991, two or more targets exploded simultaneously.

"The theory that the Iraqis could not acquire targets at ranges over 1,500 meters at night seems to have been validated by the Dreadnoughts' experience. Only Bravo Team reported multiple near misses from enemy tank fire."[3]

Further north the U.S. 1st Armored Division began to take on the doomed Republican Guard's *Medinah* Division on the evening of 27th February in a one-sided engagement that became known as the Battle of Medinah Ridge. Officers and men of the division recalled the battle for *Army Times* newspaper.

"About 7pm, tank and Bradley crew members began identifying hot spots three kilometers out and started firing. In their thermals, the crews could see Iraqi soldiers leaving their bunkers and reboarding tanks and BMP infantry vehicles. 'A lot of them were mowed down trying to get back to their vehicles,' said Maj Chess Harris, the 3rd Brigade's executive officer. But other Iraqi tanks were manned and ready for battle. He continued, 'It turned into a horrendous night fight. There was stuff going off all over the place. The fight kept going until all hot spots were burning that we could identify.'

"2nd Brigade came up against the Medinah's 2nd Brigade and about 20 minutes later was 'pretty much gone,' said Colonel Montgomery Meigs. About 60 T-72s and nine T-55s had been destroyed. The 2nd Brigade was untouched. The Iraqi division was not trying to escape, [divisional commander] *Major General Ronald Griffiths said, 'They fought very aggressively and very hard.'* But lacking the range of their American counterparts, their sights useless at the great ranges at

Below: **The Israeli LAHAT Laser Homing Anti-Tank gun-launched weapon system in action during a test. (Rafael Armaments Authority)**

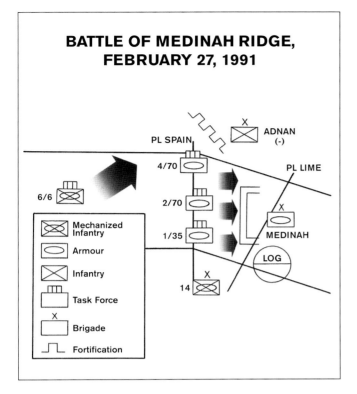

BATTLE OF MEDINAH RIDGE, FEBRUARY 27, 1991

PL SPAIN

ADNAN (-)

PL LIME

4/70

2/70

1/35

MEDINAH

LOG

6/6

14

Mechanized Infantry

Armour

Infantry

Task Force

Brigade

Fortification

which they were being engaged and their command and control targeted, the Iraqis were destroyed as if at a shooting gallery.

"'All along the ridge, you saw things that looked like blow torches,' reported Lieutenant Thomas Mundell [a Bradley commander]. 2nd Battalion, 70th Armor Regiment [2/70 Armor], in the center of the 2nd Brigade line, hit many revetted tank positions and registered hits from more than three kilometers. To the south, 1st Battalion, 35th Armor Regiment [1/35 Armor] fought elements from both the Medinah and 14th [Armored] Divisions.

"'The first seven to 10 minutes were like no Grafenwoehr [range training in Germany] I've ever seen, because each company as it came over the horizon began engaging targets to their front, and I could not visualize the length of the target that allowed so many tanks to,' says Lieutenant Colonel Jerry Wiedewitsch, commanding officer of 1st Battalion, 35th Armor Regiment. At 2,800 meters, the tankers engaged tanks.

"Specialist First Class John Scaglionne, of D Company 1/35 Armor, watched Iraqi tank turrets flip 40 feet into the air, and was dumbfounded. 'I was amazed by how much firepower we had, how much destruction we could do,' he said. 'It was a sobering thought.'

"Unable to see the U.S. tanks on the heavily overcast day, the Medinah tankers could fire only at muzzle flashes. 'You'd see tanks fire back and you'd see the rounds drop 1,000 meters short of the tanks,' Mundell said. At certain points, there were three fights underway. The close fight with tanks and Bradleys: Apaches and MLRS working targets 15 to 20 kilometers in front of them against dug-in or escaping forces, and deeper in zone air strikes against known positions.

"'You had artillery, Apaches, A-10s, tanks, the entire divisions—all the combat power we could muster—all firing and servicing the Medinah Division at the same time,' said Col V.V. Corn, the divisional artillery commander.

"The division's battle damage assessment was: 186 tanks and 127 APCs destroyed that day, including 137 vehicles in less than one hour, in one of the biggest battles of the war. 'It was surreal' says Griffiths, who observed the battle during a lightning storm on the ground behind 2nd Brigade and in front of the artillery. 'It was really an awesome spectacle which Mother Nature made even more spectacular.'"[4]

The 2nd Armored Cavalry Regiment did not have such an easy time in the Battle of 73 Easting when it found itself up against the Republican Guard's *Tawakalna* Division and 12th Armored Division.

"Sgt Larry Foltz, 2nd Squadron's combat observation lasing team sergeant, was in his fire support vehicle deployed with G Troop, trying to identify targets with his laser designator. Moving up to 73 Easting line, E and G troops picked up a major armored force, a combination of elements of the Tawakalna Division and the 12th Armored Division. The Americans halted on a ridge overlooking a wide shallow gully or wadi.

"'It was hard for me to pick targets,' said Foltz. Visibility still was atrocious. Everywhere in front vehicles were burning and munitions exploding. 'Things were getting a little frantic.' Finally the sand storm began to diminish, and Foltz found a target area. But the platoon was taking incoming tank fire. Out of a corner of his eye, Foltz saw a flash. A Bradley had been hit.

"'There was no sign of the crew,' Foltz remembers. 'We figured they were trapped inside.' Foltz and others tried to get the ramp open, finally succeeding in freeing the crew.

"As night fell, Republican Guard T-72s continued to mass, coming in groups fiercely attacking G and E troops, Foltz saw 'tanks coming over the hill like there's no tomorrow … They were fighting for their lives, trying to get out.' Foltz had a new problem. The thermal sight

in his fire support vehicle had blown out. Despite hellish fire as the regiment stood its ground against waves of Iraqi tanks, Foltz ran to a nearby Bradley and used its thermal sights to acquire targets. Since he could not get on the fire support radio network from the Bradley, he ran between vehicles to call in targets. During the six-hour battle, the G Troop fire support team directed 720 howitzer rounds. One mission prevented T-72s from overrunning C Troop's 3rd Platoon. 'DPICM [dual purpose/improved conventional munitions, a cargo or cluster round fired by 155mm artillery] *does wonders on T-72,' says Foltz.*

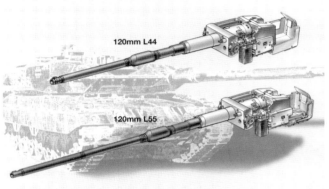

Top: **The Leopard 2A5 tank features a new L55 120mm smoothbore gun. (Rheinmetall)**

Right and Above: **Krauss Maffei Wegmann have sold the Leopard 2A5 to Sweden as the Stv 122, which features many survivability improvements. (Krauss-Maffei Wegmann)**

"By 10pm the battle had subsided. 'I didn't even remember throwing down a sleeping bag,' Foltz says. 'There was a light rain, my chemical suit was trashed and everybody's face was black.' G Troop apparently had been right in the middle of an Iraqi line of retreat." [5]

Balkan Peacekeeping

The honor of being the only UN or NATO tank unit to see action in the Balkans during the 1990s fell to the Danish Army's Leopard squadron attached to the multi-national Nordic Battalion (NORBATT) of UNPROFOR in 1994. The first crews came from the Jutland Hussars and their second-in-command, Captain Neilson, described the role of their tanks in the peacekeeping mission in Bosnia.

Below right: **The German Army's Wiesel airportable light tank has been fitted with 30mm cannons to give it added punch against lightly armored targets. (Rheinmetall)**

Below: **Many former Warsaw Pact countries have began programs to upgrade their inventories of old T-55 tanks with modern fire-control systems and armor packages.**

"A heavy tank, particularly a Leopard, is symbol. A 105mm gun fitted with a fire guidance system and a laser range finder is not that easily impressed by a drunken militiaman defending a checkpoint with a Kalashnikov. The Leopard 1 shows that we mean business." [6]

Early in March 1994, three Danish Leopards rescued a Swedish SISU armored personnel carrier that had been hit by Serb fire. While the disabled vehicle was being rescued by a Bergepanzer recovery vehicle, the Leopards provided covering fire with their heavy machine guns. A few days later, in a similar incident east of Tuzla, a squad of armored vehicles came under fire from Serb 40mm Bofors guns. A Leopard responded with 105mm fire from 3,000 yards destroying two Serb guns and killing three Serb crew members. According to Captain Nielson, the Leopards were in action very soon afterward:

"The NORBATT at Saraci built an observation post, manned mainly by Swedish soldiers, a few kilometers to the east of Tuzla airport. It was attacked often over a

period of a few weeks, and on the night of April 29, 1994, at 2200 hours, the Serbs attacked with heavy machine guns, mortars and 122mm artillery pieces. We were ordered to proceed to Saraci with our Leopard tanks, and seven tanks lumbered through the night. As the platoon neared the combat zone, two Leopards were ordered towards position Tango 2. The five remaining tanks were engaged with heavy weapons. Soon shrapnel was bouncing off their armor as 5mm, 20mm and 23mm tracers flashed across the night. A few minutes later, 89mm rockets began exploding near the tanks. It was then that the Danish commanding officer saw the tell-tale flickering flames of anti-tank missiles. He didn't think twice and ordered 'Fire!' With their infra-red scopes, the Jutland Dragoons could see their targets as clearly as daytime. We fired 72 shells with good results. Nine Serb soldiers were killed and about 20 wounded. One mortar position, one 122mm gun, several bunkers and the Sagger missile launchers were blown to bits."[7]

The UNPROFOR commander, British General Sir Michael Rose, was particularly proud of this engagement, claiming five Serb tanks were destroyed by the Danish Leopards.

Later a new contingent of Danish tank crews arrived to replace their comrades. They included a female tank gunner, Private Lize Emanuelsen, in their ranks:

"The radio cracked with the message no one wanted to hear. 'We're hit! We're hit!' came the call from the tank driver engaged in a duel with Bosnian Serb artillery and tanks. The ensuing pause was the one that seems an eternity in combat: then came relief. 'But there's no damage! Everything working normally!' The Leopard had only been grazed, the phosphorus round that struck it a glancing blow having exploded harmlessly. 'First we had an explosion 20 meters in front and then another 20 meters,' said Emanuelsen, the tank gunner. 'There was some shaking, but I couldn't feel much difference between those and the one that hit us. I think it was worse for those who heard us on the radio.'"[8]

The crew of four breathed a collective sigh of relief and got back to the deadly business at hand.

It was October 26, 1994, and at Gradacac, in the far north of Bosnia and Herzegovina, an UNPROFOR observation post manned by Swedes had been shelled by Bosnian Serb forces, forcing the soldiers to withdraw. Now they were back, this time with orders to hold their positions:

"'We got our orders to be ready to support them' said Sergeant Jens Christensen, commander of one of three tanks in the platoon deployed that day, 'The soldiers drove up to their positions and were fired at immediately, so we had to come up too.'

"The white painted tanks, unable to fire until fired on themselves, rumbled into the open, their presence intended as a warning that the observation post was to be defended. The response was not long in coming.

"'They fired at us first. That's clear' said Christensen. 'Our platoon leader had one about 10 meters away, and then he fired two warning shots with his smoke shells, but they kept on firing on him. Then he fired back, and whole battle started.'

"Emanuelsen, firing from the tank that was hit by the phosphorus round, delivered two thirds of the 21 main armament rounds sent back by the three Leopards. There was at least one direct hit on an opposing tank, and possibly a hit on a howitzer position.

"'They were firing smoke, phosphor, everything at us, and they started with heavy artillery from about 15 kilometers away, and we had to withdraw' said Christensen. 'It was pretty scary I can promise you.'"[9]

Chechnya

Russia's conflict to stamp out Muslim independence fighters in the Caucasus republic of Chechnya escalated into all-out war in December 1994. Several Russian Army divisions and special forces brigades converged on Grozny, the capital of Chechnya. This was held by bands of determined guerrilla fighters who were lying in wait with Kalashnikovs, mines, rocket propelled grenades and knives.

The Russian commander, General Anatoly Kvashnin, planned to storm the city in a multi-pronged armored attack on New Year's Eve. He described the aim of the operation:

"The operational concept at this stage provided for the assault detachments attacking from the northern, western and eastern salients, entering the city and in collaboration with the MVD [ministry of interior] and FCS [Federal Counter-intelligence Service] special sub-units, seizing the presidential palace, the government television and radio buildings, the rail road station and other important establishments in the city center."[10]

Almost as soon as the troops entered the city, the Chechens emerged from their cellars to start raining down fire on the Russian tank columns from high buildings. In the narrow streets the Russian T-72 tanks and BMPs could not elevate their main armaments or co-axial machine guns to engage the enemy, while poorly trained Russian conscript infantry cowered inside their BMPs, which were soon to be turned into metal coffins. In the chaos, Russian vehicles were trapped and could not maneuver. Many Russians abandoned their vehicles and fled on foot. "There was a crazy game of hide and seek with Russian soldiers hiding in apartments, bunkers and even toilets, and the Chechens hunting them down with swords, knives and pistols," said one journalist who witnessed the battle.

Private Sergeyev, a BMP gunner in the Maikop Brigade, which spearheaded the operation, described the debacle:

"On December 31st they ordered us into our BMPs, and we set off. We did not know where we were going, but the next morning we found ourselves by the railway station in Grozny... Then all hell broke loose. There were 260 of us there. Our commander was killed right

Left: **UK High Explosive Squash Head (HESH) is designed to smash deadly chunks off the inside of enemy armor by the force of its explosion, to kill crew members of the enemy tank. (Tim Ripley)**

Right: **French troops watch Iraqi armor burning in the Gulf War. (ECPA)**

away. We lost a lot of officers. We did not know what to do. Our armor was burning. We gathered some wounded and tried to take them out, but the tank transporting them was destroyed, too. I escaped and tried to hide in the basement of a bakery, but the wall collapsed… I don't known how many Russian soldiers died in that slaughter."[11]

The nature of the disaster that befell the 131st Maikop Brigade can be gauged by the fact it lost 20 out of 26 T-72 tanks, 102 infantry fighting vehicles and all six Tungas self-propelled anti-aircraft vehicles in a matter of minutes. Only 11 men survived. One Russian officer blamed his senior commanders for the mistakes that led to the massacre:

"Those who fought in Grozny believe Kvashnin and [General] Shevtsev are mostly to blame for the faulty

organization of the operation. When the troops entered the city, they had to protect themselves. What the generals created in Grozny is what the troops described as a 'meat combine.' There are mountains of wrecked equipment in Grozny."

During 1995 the Russians reorganized their hapless forces to take on the elusive Chechen rebels. They relied on their superior firepower to turn the republic into a huge free-fire zone. Captain Andrey Antipov described how Russian tank crews recast their tactics.

"[General] Lov Rokhlin invented a 'carousel of fire.' Its essence was to unleash a hurricane of fire against targets without allowing the enemy to raise his head. This is how it was done. A tank was driven into an emplacement, and it fired as long as there was ammunition in the automatic loader. That is 20 rounds.

Two other tanks stood nearby under cover. When it was through firing, the tank quickly came out of the emplacement, and another took its place. After that a third. Meanwhile, the first tank was reloading. The rate of fire was staggering, there were no interruptions. For a long time, the veteran Chechen fighters could not understand how there could be such fire from one point."[12]

Armored Omdurman?

The one sided nature of the 1991 Gulf War, where, as we have seen, 3,800 Iraqi tanks were destroyed for the loss of 18 U.S. tanks, confirmed the superiority of Western tanks over Soviet-designed vehicles. The casualty figures recalled the Battle of Omdurman in September 1898 where British colonial forces used massed Maxim machine guns against Sudanese tribesmen. Some 11,000 natives died and the British counted their dead by the scores. With the Gulf War, the era of almost casualty-free wars seemed to have returned for Western countries.

Yet less than four years later the Russian experience in Chechnya highlighted the fact that on many battlefields around the world, modern war is not the "video game" some pundits try to claim. There were still scores of "real wars" occurring around the world in which the protagonists were prepared to fight and die for their cause. In these conflicts the tank was still a weapon of choice.

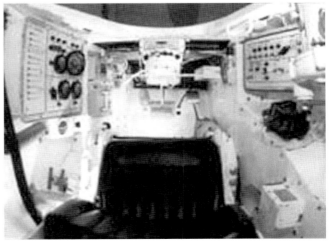

Above: **Some 3,700 Iraqi tanks were claimed destroyed by coalition forces. (MoD)**

Right: **The driver's position of an Abrams tank is a sophisticated workspace. (STRICOM)**

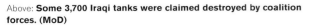

At the start of the 21st century the tank has reached a crossroads. While the 1991 Gulf War seemed to show that tanks of Western design had reached the pinnacle of their evolution as weapon systems, other trends were indicating the tank's day might have passed.

Around the world armies were happy to keep some of their existing inventories of 1980s-vintage tanks in service, and spend limited amounts of money upgrading them, but no country was contemplating designing and building new ones in the near term. Tank manufacturers in America, Britain, China, France, Germany, Italy, Israel, Japan, Russia, South Korea and the Ukraine were are all struggling to find work to keep their design teams and factories in work. Many of these countries had small scale research efforts studying future tank designs, but there were no projects that were due to go into production until late in the second decade of the 21st century, when the current generation of tanks would be worn out. It seemed that many years would elapse until these orders actually materialized, leaving factories empty and design teams idle. Export orders to countries in Asia and the Mid-East in recent years have numbered only a few hundred vehicles, further undermining the viability of the world's tank industry.

The end of the Cold War and subsequent collapse of defense spending around the world appeared to have removed the immediate demand for new products. With no prospect of war there seemed little incentive to develop new tanks to fight imaginary threats. At the same time the development of new anti-armor weapons, particularly missile-armed attack helicopters such as the AH-64D Apache Longbow, raised the possibility that the tank had at last met its match on the battlefield. There seemed little point in developing

Right: **Britain's Defence Evaluation & Research Agency (DERA) has a program to produce a demonstration vehicle, the Advanced Composite Armoured Vehicle Platform (ACAVP), with "plastic" or non-metal based armor. (DERA)**

counter-measures to this threat, when only Western countries possessed these powerful weapon systems and also boasted unrivalled air supremacy. The trend towards peacekeeping missions also mitigated against investment in tanks, as armies began refocusing their reduced procurement budgets on equipment needed for humanitarian relief, crowd control and low-intensity operations. High intensity combat on the scale of the Gulf War seemed an anachronism.

For the world's armored warriors, this gloomy state affairs was hardly inspiring. From being the cutting edge

of warfare for most of the last century, they seemed to be an endangered species in the new century.

The famous British military historian Basil Liddell Hart once said, "the only thing harder than getting a new idea into the military mind is to get an old one out." In October 1999 the U.S. Army Chief of Staff Eric K. Shinseki seemed to sound the death knell of the tank by scrapping America's programs to build new tanks and other heavy armored vehicles. Panic set in among certain parts of the U.S. Army and the American defense industry, as Shinseki rushed through

Right and Opposite page: **The U.S. Army is buying thousands of Light Armored Vehicle 3s to equip its Interim Brigades until its new Future Combat System is ready for service. (General Motors Diesel Division)**

orders to equip five airportable "Interim Force" brigades with wheeled Light Armored Vehicles (LAVs) designed by the Swiss company Mowag and made in Canada. The U.S. Army seemed to be designing totally itself for low-intensity operations in which tanks were no longer needed.

Shinseki, however, may prove to be more of a visionary than some of his critics give him credit for. The problems of moving the U.S. Army's Task Force Hawk to Albania in April 1999 at the height of the Kosovo War were the catalysts for his plan to transform every aspect of how the U.S. Army goes to war. According to Shinseki, there was little point in having superbly armored tanks with superlative firepower, if they could not be moved quickly to theaters of operation. A lack of strategic mobility was identified as the U.S. Army's Achilles heel in the 21st century.

The Interim Force is what its names implies, a stopgap, until new technology can be applied to solve the strategic mobility problem. Shinseki gutted the U.S. Army's research and development budget to find $8 billion to fund the development of the Future Combat System (FCS). The aim is to have the FCS ready to equip the first units of the so-called Objective Force by the end of the decade.

According to the U.S. Army, the FCS will be the primary weapon/troop-carrying platform for the Objective Force. It is envisaged as common platform for a variety of roles, indirect fire, direct fire, infantry carrier and sensor platform. The role of the platform is stressed more than any requirement to have tracks or a turret. The buzz-word for the FCS is "network-centric," and each platform will be able to process reconnaissance, surveillance and target-acquisition data from other platforms, higher echelon command posts or national strategic systems. By giving the FCS information superiority thanks to the "tactical internet," it will have less requirement for armor and firepower, reducing its size and weight.

The U.S. Army has set the FCS's designers very strict weight criteria. Each vehicle must be able to fit into a C-130 Hercules-sized transport aircraft. Compared to the current Abrams tank, the FCS is to be 70% lighter and 50% smaller while having the equivalent (or better) lethality and survivability. The FCS is to weigh no more than 20 tons with 300 to 400 cubic feet of internal volume. The M1 Abrams weighs 62 tons and has 650 cubic feet of internal volume. Among technologies being considered for incorporation into the FCS are an electromagnetic gun, a directed energy weapon, precision missiles using

common modular missile technologies, networked fire control and robots. Unmanned FCS platforms could perform the indirect-fire, direct-fire and sensor functions. Each FCS is to incorporate capabilities for wireless communications and sensor-data reception, and it is possible that the powerplant could use hybrid electric propulsion or fuel cells.

The aim of the project is to produce a combat force that can fight both high intensity warfare and take part in peacekeeping style operations. To do this the FCS must be able to provide the same level of protection to its crews as the current generation of U.S. tanks and armored fighting vehicles. Zero casualties are still the Pentagon's first priority. It is not the intention of the FCS program to build a "Sherman of the 21st century," a cheap and lightly armored tank that is dead-meat when put up against better protected and more lethal enemy tanks.

Not surprisingly the ability to develop dramatically improved lightweight armored protection has been identified as a key element of the FCS program. The U.S. Army says advanced ceramic armor holds promise. Armor protection could be based on active systems to defeat both chemical energy (CE) and kinetic energy (KE) threats. The mechanism to defeat CE or High Explosive Anti-Tank (HEAT) rounds could include multiple explosively formed penetrators or momentum-transfer mechanisms to defeat or disrupt KE rounds as they impact. Other options include so-called "smart armor" that directs an air blast to force the incoming KE round to miss.

Right: **GIAT Industries' concept of the future of armored warfare. (GIAT Industries)**

Below: **BAE Systems' concept of missile-armed armored vehicles. (BAE Systems)**

One of the more esoteric ideas under consideration is armor that incorporates an electric field sandwiched within it, with enough power circulating inside instantly to change the molecular structure of any round hitting it—dissipating the shaped charge jet from a HEAT round before it can penetrate the crew compartment. While U.S. Army scientists say the idea is theoretically possible, a major problem is finding a power supply small enough to meet the FCS's weight criteria. There is also a requirement to develop capacitors that would make such a system possible on a vehicle. Nevertheless, scientists believe that an electric field is not beyond the realm of possibility, and pushing the envelope is the charger of the Objective Force's science and technology effort.

Shinseki is often heard to quote the U.S. Civil War Confederate General Nathan Bedford Forrest, who supposedly coined the phrase, "get there fustest with the mostest." The aim of the Objective Force is to be able to put a combat capable brigade anywhere in the world in 96 hours, a full division in 120 hours and five divisions on the ground within 30 days. The U.S. Army

is not going to scrap its Abrams tanks and Bradley IFVs just yet. They will soldier on for at least 20 more years as second or third echelon forces, arriving by sea after the Objective Force has won the first round of any conflict.

The U.S. Army is not the only army looking at ideas for making the tank relevant to the 21st century battlefield. The United Kingdom's Defence Evaluation & Research Agency (DERA) has already built a concept demonstrator "plastic tank" which uses composite armor instead of steel plate. The British Army has the Mobile Direct Fire Equipment Requirement (MODIFIER) to follow on from the current Challenger 2 fleet after 2015. Its main application will be to destroy ground based anti-armor systems so it will require good armored protection, and there is a need to make it as light as possible for strategic mobility. It is, however, stressed that MODIFIER is not a straight tank replacement program and it may be merged with plans for a future infantry fighting vehicle to carry troops into battle. "If we can do the job in a better way we will do it that way," said a senior officer involved in the program.

Although the British Army employs different terminology to its American cousins, FCS and MODIFIER have evolved through the same thought processes and give some indication of the state of current military thinking on the future of the tank.

In the 85 years since the tank first emerged on the bloody battlefields of the Western Front, it has gone through many evolutions. Although there is much debate about radical alternatives to the tank, many of these ideas and views are not new. People have predicted the demise of the tank, almost from the day it first went into action. The concept of a heavily protected armored vehicle, capable of cross country movement and carrying potent firepower, has proved itself time and again on numerous battlefields. It would be a brave man who predicted that such a weapon system was obsolete. Indeed, to paraphrase a famous quote, "if the tank did not exist, you would have to invent it."

Above: **Night vision systems are an integral part of modern armored vehicles. 21st century tanks are provided with a wide array of sensors to detect their targets. They range from thermal imaging night vision devices in the turret, electro-optical daytime observation devices and simple optical vision blocks. The fielding of defensive aid systems opens up new possibilities to fit sensors to tanks, including laser detectors to pinpoint when they are being swept by laser target designators, radars to spot incoming anti-tank missiles, aircraft or helicopters, heat sensors to detect missile exhausts and sound detectors to pick up helicopter rotor noise. In extreme circumstances the tank commander can still open his turret and use his Mark One Eyeball to look for targets.**

Left: **Modern tank designs and concepts are tested in virtual wargames to gain data on the performance of their weapon systems.**

Far left: **Modern tanks take shape first as computer generated models before they proceed to production. (C2G)**

Top: **Ease of use and cheapness are an essential part of modern tank design.**

Above: **21st century tanks are all connected to via "tactical internets" to ensure commanders have total "situational awareness" of what both friendly and enemy forces are doing on the battlefield. (GIAT Industries)**

Right: **The UK-U.S. TRACER/Future Scout Combat Systems (FSCS) is an example of the type of armored fighting vehicles being developed in the first decade of the 21st century. (BAE Systems)**

Over page: **Leclerc firing on the move. (GIAT Industries)**

Ron Natividad 8-21-98

Below and Below left: **The Advanced Composite Armoured Vehicle Platform (ACAVP), with "plastic" or non-metal based armor as compared to the current British IFV, Warrior. (DERA)**

Right: **The French main battle tank Leclerc.**

REFERENCES

World War I
1. A.J. Smithers, *Cambrai*, pp. 90–1
2. Hugh Ellis, Special Order No 6, original in Tank Museum, Bovington
3. Original account in Tank Museum, Bovington
4. A.J. Smithers, *Cambrai*, p. 110
5. A.J. Smithers, *Cambrai*, pp. 119–20
6. A.J. Smithers, *Cambrai*, p. 137
7. Carlo D'Este, *A Genius For War*, p. 233
8. Carlo D'Este, *A Genius For War*, p. 256

World War II
1. Thomas Jentz, *Panzer Truppen*, Vol 1, pp. 122–3
2. David Rissik, *The DLI at War*, pp. 25–6
3. Thomas Jentz, *Panzer Truppen*, Vol 1, p. 204
4. Helmut Ritgen, *The 6th Panzer Division*, pp. 28–32
5. Dal McGuirk, *Rommel's Army in Africa*, pp. 80–81
6. Thomas Jentz, *Panzer Truppen*, Vol 1, pp. 164–5
7. David Fletcher, *Crusader*, p. 22
8. Masanobu Tsuji, *Japan's Greatest Victory, Britain's Worse Defeat*, pp. 95–8
9. Merrill B Twining, *No Bended Knee*, p. 130
10. Pavel Rotmistrov, *Tanks against Tanks*, pp.113–15
11. Rudolf Lehman, *The Leibstandarte*, p. 235
12. Rudolf Lehman, *The Leibstandarte*, p. 237
13. John Foley, *Mailed Fist*, Granada Publishing, p. 14
14. Paul Carrell, *Invasion—They're Coming!*, pp. 150, 153
15. Ken Trout, *Tank!*, pp. 104–5
16. Kenneth Jordan, *Yesterday's Heroes*, pp. 351–2
17. S.L.A. Marshall, *Bastogne: The First Eight Days*, pp. 56–8

Cold War
1. Anon., *Israel's Armor in Action*, pp. 53–5
2. Anon., *Israel's Armor in Action*, p. 49
3. Charles T. Kemps, *The History of the Vietnam War*, pp. 126–8
4. Donn A. Starry, *Armored Combat in Vietnam*, pp. 172–4
5. Keith W. Nolan, *Into Cambodia*, pp. 140–1
6. Robert Dorr, *Air War South Vietnam*, p. 130
7. Anon., *Israel's Armor in Action*, pp. 66–71
8. Rafael Eitan, "Valley of Tears," *The Elite*, Issue 6, Volume 1
9. Ze'ev Schiff and Ehud Ya'ari, *Israel's Lebanon War*, pp. 160–1
10. Robert Fisk, *Pity the Nation: Lebanon at War*, p. 215
11. Ze'ev Schiff and Ehud Ya'ari, *Israel's Lebanon War*, pp. 178–9
12. Robert Fisk, *Pity the Nation: Lebanon at War*, pp. 227–8
13. Martin Horseman, "Canadian Army Trophy 1991," *Armed Forces*, Issue 13, pp. 16–23

New World Disorder
1. Anon., *The Hawk*, 1991, p. 108
2. Anon., *The Hawk*, 1991, pp. 123–8
3. Gregory Fontenot, "Fright Night," *Military Review*, January 1993, pp. 38–52
4. Steve Vogel, "Metal Rain," *Army Times*, 16 September 1991
5. Steve Vogel, "A Swift Kick," *Army Times*, 5 August 1991
6. Sam Katz and Yves Debay, *The Blue Helmets Under Fire*, pp. 57–8
7. Ibid.
8. Richard Calver, "Leopards on the prowl support cause of peace," *UNPROFOR News*, December 1994, p. 10
9. Ibid.
10. John F. Antalm, "A Glimpse of Wars to Come: The Battle for Grozny," *Army*, June 1999, pp. 28–40
11. Ibid
12. Ibid

BIBLIOGRAPHY

Official Documents
The Biggest war in the Mid-East, Born in Battle, Hod Hasharon, 1978
Conduct of the Persian Gulf War, U.S. Department of Defense, Washington DC, 1992
German Reports Series, 18 Volumes, U.S. Army
The Hawk, Regimental Journal of the 14th/20th King's Hussars, Preston, 1991
History of World War II, Purnell & Sons, 1966–74
Israel's Armour in Action, Born in Battle, Hod Hasharon, 1978
Records of the Wehrmacht Inspector of Panzer Troops

Books
John F. Antalm, "A Glimpse of Wars to Come: The Battle for Grozny," *Army*, Arlington, June 1999
Richard Armstrong, *The Armored Guards: Red Army Tank Commanders*, Schiffer Military History, Atglen, 1994
Ray Bonds, *The Soviet War Machine*, Salamander Books, London, 1980
Chris Bishop, *WWII: The Directory of Weapons*, Aerospace Publishing, London, 2000
Paul Carrell, *Invasion—They're Coming!*, George Harrap, London 1964
Richard Calver, "Leopards on the prowl support cause of peace," *UNPROFOR News*, Zagreb, December 1994
Matthew Cooper and James Lucas, *Panzer*, Macdonald, London, 1976
Matthew Cooper and James Lucas, *Panzergrenadier*, Macdonald and Jane's, London, 1977
Robin Cross, *Citadel: The Battle of Kursk*, Michael O'Mara, London, 1993
Duncan Crow, *U.S. Armor-Cavalry*, Profile Publishing, Windsor, 1973
Duncan Crow and Robert J. Icks, *Encyclodpedia of Tanks*, Barrie & Jenkins, London, 1975
Robert Dorr, *Air War South Vietnam*, Arms and Armour, London, 1990
James Dunnigan, *The Russian Front*, Arms and Armour, London, 1978
Roger Edwards, *Panzer: A Revolution in Warfare, 1939-45*, Arms and Armour, London, 1989
Rafael Eitan, "Valley of Tears," Issue 6, Volume 1, *The Elite*, Orbis, London, 1985
Carlo D'Este, *A Genius For War*, Harper Collins, London 1996
Robert Fisk, *Pity the Nation: Lebanon at War*, Oxford Paperbacks, Oxford, 1990
David Fletcher, *The Great Tank Scandal*, HMSO, London, 1989
David Fletcher, *Crusader*, Osprey, London, 1995
David Fletcher, *Matilda*, Osprey, London, 1994
John Foley, *Mailed Fist*, Panther Books, London 1957
Gregory Fontenot, "Fright Night," *Military Review*, Fort Leavenworth, January 1993
George Forty, *German Tanks of World War II*, Blandford Press, London, 1987
Chris Foss, *Jane's AFV Recognition Handbook*, Jane's Information Group, London, 1992
Marsh Gelbart, *Tanks*, Brassey's, London, 1996
Heinz Guderian, *Panzer Leader*, Futura, London, 1979
Peter Gudgin, *Armoured Firepower*, Sutton Publishing, Stroud, 1997
Paddy Griffiths, *Battle Tactics of the Western Front*, Yale University Press, New Haven, 1994
Martin Horseman, "Canadian Army Trophy 1991," *Armed Forces*, Issue 13, Ian Allan, Shepperton, 1981
Thomas Jentz, Hilary Doyle, Peter Sarson, *Tiger I*, Osprey, London, 1993
Thomas Jentz, *Panzer Truppen*, Vol 1 & 2, Schiffer Military History, Atglen, 1996
Kenneth Jordan, *Yesterday's Heroes*, Schiffer Military History, Atglen, 1996
Sam Katz and Yves Debay, *The Blue Helmets Under Fire*, Concord, Hong Kong, 1996
Sam Katz, *Merkava*, Osprey, London, 1997
Sam Katz, *Israeli Tank Battles*, Arms and Armour, London, 1988
Charles T. Kemps, *The History of the Vietnam War*, Aerospace Publishing 1988
Egon Kleine and Volkmar Kuhn, *Tiger*, Motorbuch Verlag, Stuttgart
Rudolf Lehman, *The Leibstandarte*, JJ Fedorowicz, Manitoba, 1990
Kenneth Macksey, *Tank versus Tank*, Grub Street, London, 1988
S.L.A. Marshall, *Bastogne: The First Eight Days*, Center of U.S. Military History, U.S. Army, Washington DC, 1996
Dal McGuirk, *Rommel's Army in Africa*, Century Hutchinson, London, 1987
Stan Morse, *Gulf Air War Debrief*, Aerospace Publishing, London, 1991
Keith W. Nolan, *Into Cambodia*, Dell Books, 1990
Nigel Pearce, *The Shield and the Sabre*, HMSO, 1992
Tim Ripley, *Steel Storm*, Sutton Publishing, Stroud, 2000
David Rissik, *The DLI at War*, The Durham Light Infantry, Durham, 1952
Helmut Ritgen, *The 6th Panzer Division*, Osprey, London, 1982
Pavel Rotmistrov, *Tanks against Tanks*, Voenizdat, Moscow, 1984
General Sir Michael Rose, *Fighting For Peace*, Harvill, London, 1998
Uwe Schnellbacher and Michael Jerchel, *Leopard 2*, Osprey, London, 1998
General Fridio von Senger und Etterlin, *Neither Fear nor Hope*, Greenhill, London, 1989
Ze'ev Schiff and Ehud Ya'ari, *Israel's Lebanon War*, Counterpoint, London, 1984
A.J. Smithers, *Cambrai*, Leo Cooper, London, 1992
Donn A. Starry, *Armoured Combat in Vietnam*, Blandford Press, Poole, 1980
John Terraine, *White Heat: New Warfare 1914-1918*, Leo Cooper, London, 1982
Ken Trout, *Tank!*, Robert Hale, London, 1985
Peter Tsouras, *Changing Orders*, Arms and Armour, London, 1994
Masanobu Tsuji, *Japan's Greatest Victory, Britain's Worse Defeat*, Spellmount, Staplehurst, 1997
Merrill B. Twining, *No Bended Knee*, Presidio, Novato, 1996
Steve Vogel, "Metal Rain," *Army Times*, Springfield, 16 September 1991
Steve Vogel, "A Swift Kick," *Army Times*, Springfield, 5 August 1991
Steve Zaloga, *T-72*, Osprey, London, 1993
Steve Zaloga, *M1 Abrams*, Osprey, London, 1993
Steve Zaloga, *T-34/76*, Osprey, London, 1994
Steve Zaloga and Kim Kinnear, *T-34/85*, Osprey, London, 1996
Steve Zaloga, *IS-2*, Osprey, London, 1994
Steve Zaloga, *Sherman*, Osprey, London, 1978
Niklas Zetterling, *Normandy 1944*, J.J. Fedorowicz, Manitoba, 2000

INDEX